CHRIST'S POOR MEN

THE CARTHUSIANS IN ENGLAND

Glyn Coppack dedicates
his parts of this book to the memory of Sue Garnett,
a dear friend, one-time custodian at Mount Grace, and chatelaine of Mount Lodge,
the home grange. who died before he began
writing the book she said he must
write if only for her.

CHRIST'S POOR MEN

THE CARTHUSIANS IN ENGLAND

GLYN COPPACK & MICK ASTON

TEMPUS

First published 2002

PUBLISHED IN THE UNITED KINGDOM BY:
Tempus Publishing Ltd
The Mill, Brimscombe Port
Stroud, Gloucestershire GL5 2QG

PUBLISHED IN THE UNITED STATES OF AMERICA BY:
Tempus Publishing Inc.
2A Cumberland Street
Charleston, SC 29401

British Library Cataloguing in Publication Data.
A catalogue record for this book is available from the British Library.

ISBN 0 7524 1961 7

Typesetting and origination by Tempus Publishing.
PRINTED AND BOUND IN GREAT BRITAIN.

Contents

List of illustrations

Text figures

Colour plates

Preface

Mick Aston and I came to study the Carthusians by very different routes; he because he was fascinated by the plethora of monastic reforms that appeared in the late eleventh and early twelfth centuries, I because I was invited to complete an unfinished research excavation at Mount Grace Priory in Yorkshire, the best-preserved English Carthusian monastery. Initially, I agreed to do only one season's work because I was deeply involved with research at Fountains Abbey, but somehow I was persuaded to stay for a further five years, though I managed to stay away in 1996-97. There is something compulsive about the Carthusians and something very special about their monasteries.

Mick is, of course, a landscape archaeologist, taking a broad view of developments while I am a digger and theorist, sometimes rather too close to the evidence to make much sense of it. We had before us an almost untouched subject which Mick approached from its origins while I excavated a later medieval Carthusian monastery – literally we were attacking our subject from both ends, aware of what each other was doing but separated by 250 miles. As with all good collaborations it required a catalyst to encourage us to work together; Philip Rahtz who united us when he brought Mick to Mount Grace in 1990.

It was Mick who collated the study of all the English charterhouses, as Carthusian monasteries are known, drawing in Paul Everson, then of the Royal Commission on Historical Monuments for England. Paul and his specialist teams of surveyors carried out detailed surveys of all the surviving sites, something possible for an order as scattered as the Carthusians but difficult for any other order in England, and commissioned geophysical surveys of them. The intention was, and still remains, for the three of us to publish an academic account of the Carthusian settlement of Britain, and so we all undertook to continue our research. Life is never as simple as that. Full time employment and other research interests inevitably get in the way of our best intentions, and a project that began in the early 1990s is still continuing. This book aims to show how far we have got in the first ten years of our collaboration. It is the first overall study of the Carthusians in England since 1930; it places what we know about Carthusian charterhouses in the context of medieval monasticism generally, and it identifies for the first time how Carthusian monasteries were developed and how their communities lived. Our perspective is archaeological, where earlier studies have been largely historical and spiritual.

We started out knowing that the Carthusians were different to other monks; that their monasteries had a plan that was very different to that of the communal orders; and that the life-style of hermits who intentionally sought anonymity would be difficult to recover. What became apparent quite rapidly was that the Carthusians were only different to other monks in some respects, while in others there were a great many similarities to the generality of other orders, and that it was defining the differences that was our challenge.

Inevitably, this book is often a digest of other people's work, though the spin put on it is our own, and we are grateful for our colleagues permission to publish their work whether it has already appeared in print of not. Without the contribution of Paul Everson and his surveyors, and Geophysical Surveys of Bradford, our knowledge of the extent and plan of all English charterhouses would be extremely limited. Laurence Keen and Andrew Saunders, whose work at Mount Grace has been funda-mental to the understanding of that site, have allowed us to use their work, which is written up but not yet published, to the full, and Iain Soden and Coventry City Museums have also let us use their material, post publication, to understand the development of the Coventry charterhouse. Jackie Hall's work on the architectural development of Mount Grace, the first detailed study in Europe of medieval Carthusian architecture, is also used before full publication, and as always Simon Hayfield and Judith Dobie have provided many of the illustrations used here.

Many of my ideas on the development of Mount Grace, which is the critical site for the study of the order in England, have been developed since 1985 in conversa-tion with Laurence Keen whose own pioneering excavation there in 1968-74 was one of the finest pieces of work ever carried out on any monastic site. His generosity and constructive criticism have ensured that a remarkably full story can be told. Similarly, Dr Allan Hall, Dr Andrew Jones, and Brian Irvine have defined the Carthusian diet, and Dr Colin Hayfield has identified the suite of pottery used by individual monks, all firsts in monastic archaeology.

Others have also contributed. Behind my comments on Carthusian architecture are hidden the offerings made to monastic architecture by Professor Peter Fergusson and Stuart Harrison; through his understanding of Carthusian history and spirituality a monk of St Hugh's charterhouse at Parkminster brought accuracy and insight to my own understanding of it; and Dr Christopher Young persuaded me to forsake the Cistercians for the archaeology of a very different order. As always, my colleagues at English Heritage have been generous in their support, and if Rod Giddins and Dr Anthony Streeten had not arranged time for the writing up of my excavations at Mount Grace (another first), this book could never have been written.

This study, which cannot be the final word, is intended to restore the Carthusians to the first rank of the reforming orders in England. Their contribution to the monastic church at a time of remarkable change, and their flowering in the later Middle Ages had dramatic effects that are still apparent, and the order is one which continues to grow across the world, with a rule which has never been reformed for it was never deformed.

Glyn Coppack
Goxhill
March 2002

1   Carthusian origins

Rheims Cathedral was probably a quiet studious place in the middle of the eleventh century, the sort of place where a cleric could have a comfortable life away from the grind of everyday existence. Bruno Hartenfaust, a Frenchman, had been born around 1032 near Cologne. Following a brief career as a canon of St Cunibert's, Cologne, he had been appointed in 1056, at the age of 24, lecturer in grammar and theology in the cathedral school at Rheims. As a portent of future events, one of his pupils was Oddone (or Eudes) de Châtillon, who became Pope Urban II in 1088 and launched the First Crusade in 1096. As we shall see, he was to have a great affect on Bruno's life.

In 1074 Bruno was appointed chancellor of the diocese of Rheims by its archbishop, Manasses, but although clearly a very able administrator, after a while he left for Cologne. He decided to become a monk, meeting Robert of Molesme, the founder (in 1098) of the Cistercian order of monks in the forests of Burgundy, where in the late eleventh century there were numerous groups of hermits living in isolated sites.

Why had Bruno decided to change his lifestyle so dramatically? What was happening in the Church in the eleventh century? In fact his move from the relative comfort and security of the cathedral precincts to the uncertain, ascetic life of the hermit-monk reflected a widespread phenomenon of the Church in the eleventh and twelfth centuries. He was merely one of a group of outstanding churchmen who in a generation or so changed the face of the Catholic Church forever, establishing the new orders of monks and canons whose names are now so familiar to us: Cistercians, Premonstratensians, Victorines, Arrouasians and Bruno's own order – the Carthusians.

Tenth-century developments

Monasticism was at a low ebb in Europe at the beginning of the tenth century. Not only had there been considerable disruption throughout the previous century, particularly by the Vikings, but many former monasteries had either become or reverted to secular establishments of clerks and priests. This process of relative decay began to be reversed with the establishment of new centres of monastic spirituality at Cluny in 909, Brogne around 930 and Gorze in 959. Cluny (in Burgundy) in particular proved to be a monastic powerhouse, and during the next couple of centuries under a succession of extremely able and long-lived abbots became a very rich, powerful and influential abbey with a vast 'empire' of dependent priories all over France and adjacent countries. Other areas also enjoyed the reform movement in the tenth century, for instance Normandy with the (re-)foundation of a number of Benedictine abbeys which became very rich and famous: Caen, Fécamp, St Wandrille and Jumiège. In England, Glastonbury Abbey was re-founded by Dunstan in 940, Abingdon and Ramsey a little later, and then a great many in the reign of King Edgar in the 960s. By 1086, when we can see their estates listed in the folios of Domesday Book, many of these tenth-century Benedictine abbeys had become incredibly wealthy with vast land holdings, often over several counties.

A reaction in the monastic world to all this wealth, power and influence was perhaps inevitable; it has been said that a reform of monasticism is necessary every two centuries or so, and in this period it came from hermits looking to the ideals of the Desert Fathers of Egypt and Syria. There was a feeling that the wealth of the Church, with the comfortable and well-fed lifestyle of the religious, was not only *not* what monks should be doing: it was ultimately bad for the soul. An ascetic life, living in the 'desert' to seek a closer affinity with God away from the affairs of men was seen by the late eleventh century to be a very desirable aim. It was of course in many ways the exact opposite of the sort of life being lived in many of the larger Benedictine and Cluniac houses of Western Europe. Within magnificent domestic accommodation, with a more than ample diet, the monks of these houses spent their days not with the mixture of worship, sleep and manual work prescribed by the Rule of St Benedict, but in an endless round of services, liturgy and increasingly elaborate rituals. By exchanging the life of a canon at Rheims for the life of a hermit in the forests of Burgundy, Bruno was responding to the spirit of the age as well as the needs of his own spirituality.

The new hermits

We can trace the origins of the new monastic lifestyles to the forested mountainous 'desert' of the Italian Appenines. After studying the lives and writings of the Desert Fathers, in 999 Romuald of Ravenna (950-1027) left the Cluniac monastery of St Apollinare-in-Classe, where he had been abbot since 996, with the aim of living like the monks in the solitude and severity of Egyptian monasteries. Wandering through central and northern Italy and the Pyrenees, founding hermitages, he eventually came to Camaldoli in Tuscany. Here in 1009, when he was around 60 years old, he founded the Hermitage of St Saviour on a wooded hillside where monks could live as hermits with the support of a community. The site is 700m above sea level, 9 km north of Arrezo. The monastery, which still survives, consists of a group of small houses, where the monks live and pray, surrounded by a wall. They meet for the liturgy in the church but rarely for meals or other communal activities. In order to train people for this severe life, Romuald founded a Benedictine monastery in the valley below Camoldoli where, by following the Benedictine Rule strictly, monks could be prepared for the eremitical life in the monastery above. This echoes John Cassian's idea, derived from Egypt and Syria in the fifth century and applied in Lérins, Marseilles, and the monasteries of

Provence, that monks needed to be spiritually prepared in the monastery for the later 'struggle' in the hermitage.

John Gualbert (995-1073), who was younger than Romuald but like him had been a Cluniac monk (at San Miniato del Monte, Florence), came to Camaldoli, and after a period of instruction left in 1029 to found Vallombrosa, a strictly contemplative Benedictine monastery near Florence. The aim, as with so many of these groups, was to create the conditions for a more austere and contemplative life, in poverty and silence, within the seclusion of the enclosed precinct. Building on a practice which existed already in a few Benedictine monasteries, John established a separate group of brethren, the lay brethren or 'conversi', to look after the practical needs of the monks (who were not permitted to carry out any manual labour). These lay brethren also acted as the link with the outside world beyond the monastic walls.

Peter Damian (1006-72), who had been abbot since 1043 at the reformed Camaldolese monastery of Fonte Avellana which he joined in 1035, was a great propagandist for the eremitical lifestyle, regarding it as the only proper life for a Christian. He became a cardinal and bishop of Ostia in 1057 and took a prominent part in the reforms of the Catholic Church undertaken during the time of Pope Gregory VII (1073-85) – the Gregorian Reform. He travelled extensively in Germany and France, and no doubt his ideas were widely broadcast.

The early Carthusians

Bruno, therefore, lived at a propitious time. Not only was the idea of living as a hermit attached to a community catching on as a way of life, following the ways of the Fathers of Egypt and Syria with their deserts translated to the mountains and forests of Western Europe, but the means for doing this had been devised at Camoldoli and Vallombrosa. He surely would have been aware of these developments, if not while he was in Rheims, certainly by the time he met Robert of Molesme, and others who were to be the earliest Cistercians, in the forests and marshes of Burgundy. This must have been around 1080, when he was about 48, because he seems to have spent three or four years as a hermit in the forests at Sèche Fontaine near Langres in Burgundy.

With six companions, Bruno eventually came to the city of Grenoble (**colour plate 1**), at the foothills of the Alps. Here the local bishop (St) Hugh was sympathetic to Bruno's ideas and helped the small group to establish their hermitage in a remote, mountainous area of the French Alps called Chartreuse (also known earlier as Chatrousse or Caruse) in 1084 **(1)**. It was a significant event for Western Europe. This was the first of the 'mother houses' of the important new monastic and religious orders which were to dominate the western Church for the next five centuries. All the others came later, even if their founders were already active, living as hermits and developing sites for their followers. Cîteaux (from which the name 'Cistercians' was derived) was founded by Robert of Molesme in the marshes and woods near Nuit St Georges in Burgundy in 1098, Tiron (the Tironensians) by Bernard near Chartres

1 *St Bruno's chapel and well, on the original site of La Chartreuse in the French Alps*

in 1109, Savigny (the Savigniacs) by Vitalis in the forests between Normandy and Brittany in 1112, Prémontré (the Premonstratensians) by Norbert in Picardie in 1120 and Grandmont (the Grandmontines) by Stephen at Muret in the forests near Limoges in 1124.

The new group of Bruno's followers who became the Carthusians incorporated ideas developed at Camaldoli and Vallombrosa, and no doubt elsewhere, into their way of life. This attracted monks who would live as hermits in their own cells, carrying out services there and eating and sleeping as if in a hermitage. They were expected to carry out some form of manual labour – some had a workshop, others had gardens. These 'fathers' were in turn supported by lay brethren – the 'frères' who lived in a separate monastery and did the manual work, such as farming and cutting firewood, to help in supporting the hermits. Each of these ideas, as we have seen, had already been developed elsewhere, but it was here at La Grande Chartreuse that they were combined most successfully.

The site in Chartreuse chosen by Bruno for his hermitage is spectacular. At 1180m up in the pré-Alps near a col (Col de la Ruchère), above a flat plateau surrounded by sheer vertical limestone walls and only accessible through a narrow gulley (later Porte de l'Enclos), buildings were put up to house the small community. The focal point is a spring, St Bruno's well, under a cliff and stone outcrop. Next to this is a terrace, the only flat land for miles around, though it is not clear whether any levelling was carried out before the buildings were erected. On top of the cliff is the much-altered chapel of St Bruno, which is said to incorporate the earliest church on the site. Nearby the church of Notre Dame de Casalibus marks the site of the great cloister and the cells (**2**). There is a cemetery nearby.

2 *The church of Notre-Dame de Casalibus on the site of the original Chartreuse in the French Alps*

A long way below the other half of the monastery, the 'lower house' or ' correrie', was built near the entrance to the plateau for the lay brethren. This arrangement whereby the 'fathers' – the hermits – in the 'upper house' were separated from the 'brothers' in the 'lower house' was the common layout for the earliest Carthusian monasteries. As we shall see, it was employed at the first two Carthusian priories in England, at Witham (founded 1178-9) and Hinton (1227), both in Somerset, and both of which had 'lower houses' or 'correries' which were each significantly still called 'Friary' (for 'frerie' – brothers). There was probably a 'lower house' at the short-lived Irish house of Kinaleghin (*c.* 1252- c 1321/1341) in County Galway, and also at the failed house of Hatherop (1222 to 1227/32) in Gloucestershire. However, by the time that Beauvale in Nottinghamshire was founded in 1343, the idea of lower houses had been abandoned; although the monasteries still had lay brethren, they were now housed within the same enclosure as the fathers.

We know what the original Bruno charterhouse looked like because we have the descriptions of two contemporary travellers, curious visitors who had clearly gone there to see what was going on. In 1104 Abbot Guibert of Nogent visited the site and mentioned the cells of the monks lying around the cloister, the classic distinguishing feature of the plan of a Carthusian monastery. A little later, in 1126, Peter the Venerable, while he was abbot of Cluny (he lived from about 1092 to 1156) described the site as like the early Egyptian *laura* plan, which implies again an open space with the cells around it. These are important observations, not only because they show us that almost from the beginning the monastic plan of these sites seems to have been worked out in some detail, but also because, in the case of La Grande Chartreuse, the site of the main monastery was later moved.

A new order

As with the Cistercians, it does not seem to have been the intention of Bruno to found a new monastic order; that idea, and the formal papal mechanism for permitting and recognizing new orders, came along later. At Cîteaux it was not until a decade or so after the original 'new monastery' had been founded (in 1098) that additional daughter houses were developed (La Ferté 1113, Pontigny 1114, Clairvaux 1115 and Morimond 1115). The 'Cistercian Rule', the *Carta Caritatis* came later as well, written by Stephen Harding, formerly an English monk at the cathedral monastery of Sherborne in Dorset. It is also generally thought that the entry of Bernard (of Fontaines, later of Clairvaux) to Cîteaux with many of his relatives in 1112 was a great fillip to the development of the monastery as the head house of a separate order, a status recognised by the pope around 1119. In many ways, Stephen Harding and Bernard of Clairvaux were the real 'founders' of the 'order', rather than Robert of Molesme who was the founder of the mother house (admittedly no mean achievement in its own right).

So it was with the Chartreuse. Bruno was called away in 1090 to Rome by his former student from Rheims who two years earlier had become pope (Urban II) to act as advisor. New foundations, as we shall see, did not begin to be made until 1115, some 30 years after the original foundation. And the 'Rule' for the initial group of Carthusian monasteries, the *consuetudines cartusiae*, was not written until around 1127 by the fifth prior of La Grande Chartreuse, Guigo or Guigues de St-Romain (1083-1136).

While in Rome, Bruno lived as a hermit in the ruins of the baths of Diocletian, but the second house to be founded by him was really La Torre in Calabria (Italy) to which he was allowed to retreat in 1191. He never went back to La Grande Chartreuse, though he did correspond with the monks there and advise them on their way of life, until his death at La Torre in 1101 aged around 70.

In 1132 the monastery at La Grande Chartreuse was destroyed by an avalanche, which wrecked buildings and killed some of the monks. Guigues decided to move the site to a lower location, midway between the old site and the correrie, and this is where the present monastery is situated (**3**). It is still in a spectacular position, on a bench on the valley side surrounded by sheer limestone cliffs and pine forests. The core of the present buildings, a cloister with cells around, a church and chapter house, was developed at this time. It was later extended to a double house in 1324 and a triple house in 1595, with additional cloisters built in line along the mountainside. Much larger buildings were later added to accommodate visiting priors from the other charterhouses of Europe, who arrived each September for the annual General Chapter.

The expansion and development of the order came about as a result of Guigues, the fifth prior. He had joined the community at the age of 23 in 1106 and three years later, on the death of prior Jean de Toscane, the other monks elected him prior, a post he was to retain until his death in 1136 at the age of 53 years. During this long period Guigues achieved a lot. In 1133 the Cathusians

3 *The present Carthusian monastery at La Grande Chartreuse at the site selected by Guigues in 1132*

were accepted by the papacy as a separate group or 'order' within the Benedictines. He not only effectively wrote the 'Rule' of the new group, as we have seen, and relocated the site after the avalanche, but he was also instrumental in establishing the first group of 'daughter' hermitages of La Grande Chartreuse. These were mainly in the Alps, though quickly the idea caught on in other areas. So rather like the situation with the Cistercians, though Bruno was the founder, it was Guigues who developed the groups of hermits in the Alps in the early twelfth century into a well-organised order (**4**).

The first charterhouses

There is some disagreement and doubt about which monasteries should be included in the first foundations. Les Portes (**5**) was established in 1115, and 1116 saw the foundation of first Les Ecouges, then Durbon, La Sylve Bénite and finally Meyriat. There is really no debate among scholars about the existence and the order of these. The 'official' history of the order then has Arvières (1132) and Le Mont-Dieu (1134) as the next two charterhouses to be founded. Other accounts, however, include the sites at St Sulpice en Bugey (founded 1116), Montrieux (1117), 'Aiaunus' (?1135), Vallon (1137/8) and Vaucluse (1139) before Le Mont-Dieu.

This confused situation is compounded by a number of the earliest houses changing their sites after relatively short periods of occupation. As we have seen, La Grande Chartreuse was resited after the avalanche of 1132. But Les Portes was also

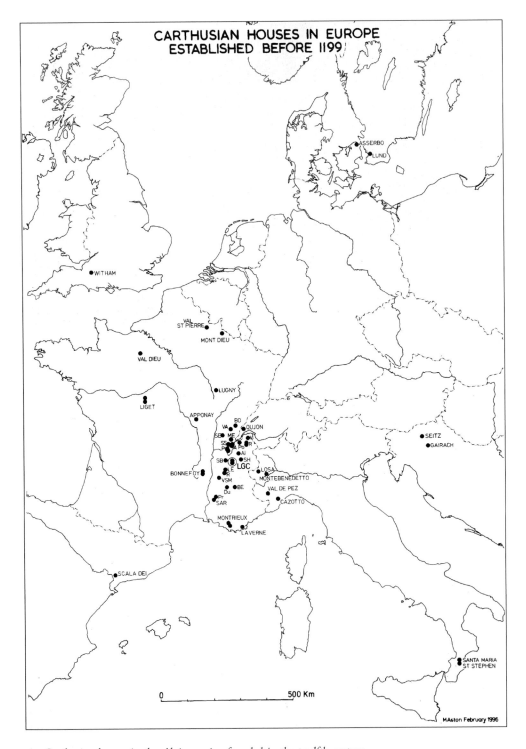

4 *Carthusian houses in the Alpine region founded in the twelfth century*

5 *Les Portes Charterhouse, established in 1115 in the French Alps*

relocated; the original site, which became the correrie (**5**), was only occupied for ten years before the present monastery higher up the mountain was established in 1125. Montrieux (now called le Vieux – the 'old') was occupied until 1170 before the present site (Montrieux le Jeune) was adopted. Like Les Portes, Arvières was only occupied for ten years, at a valley site called la Cimitière, before a fire destroyed it. A new site was chosen for rebuilding 2km to the south, on a spectacular southward projecting peninsula with steep forested valleys all around. The removal of a village in 1168 at La Sylve Bénite was probably something to do with the development of the Carthusian site.

While Meyriat and La Sylve Bénite seem to have stayed on their original sites the longest, through to their dissolution at the time of the French Revolution in the 1790s, these early relocations mean that there are some original sites with relatively intact archaeology which may be undisturbed by later building campaigns, an aspect which does not seem to have been realised in French archaeological circles. Each of these early sites would have had a correrie no more than a few kilometres away from the mother house. In some cases these have survived, and as we have seen with Les Portes the roles of the upper and lower houses might be reversed. How often did this happen in the earliest days of the life of these monasteries?

Another occurence that can lead to confusion is a monastery which is abandoned by the Carthusians, and subsequently adopted by another order. This may explain 'Aiaunus' which possibly became the Cistercian abbey of 'Buzay', and is certainly the most likely explanation for St Sulpice en Bugey. This was clearly a Carthusian monastery from 1115/16 (or possibly 1123) to around 1133. It is a spectacular site, high

6 *The ruins of the correrie chapel at Les Portes, on the site of the earlier charterhouse*

up in mountain meadows and a riot of alpine flowers in the summer. However, it is clear that the community at St Sulpice, for whatever reason, decided around 1133 to become part of the Cistercian order of monasteries, which at that time was enjoying a phenomenal period of expansion under the influence of the charismatic Bernard of Clairvaux. The early Carthusians seem to have been so angry or upset by this change of allegiance that St Sulpice en Bugey is not acknowledged as one of their earliest sites. Other charterhouses were abandoned, and only resettled by different groups later on. Les Ecouges was abandoned in 1294 to be replaced by a community at Revesti, and Durbon, failing in 1178, was revived as a monastery of Carthusian nuns in 1446 at nearby Bertaud on an amazing, remote site in the Alps behind Provence.

If we look at this first generation of Carthusian monasteries in Europe up to the time of the death of Guigues (1136) or the first General Chapter of the order (1140), we can see that there are about 20 sites (see table opposite).

Is there a typical location for a Carthusian monastery? First impressions today suggest that remote isolated situations were chosen, locally inaccessible or at least only able to be reached with considerable difficulty or discomfort, hemmed in by mountains and surrounded by alpine pine forests (**6**). Closer examination, however, reveals inevitably a more complex picture. The factors of isolation and remoteness were no doubt largely true in the middle ages – this after all was what the hermits of these monasteries were interested in. But with a dozen or so 'fathers' and however many 'brothers' supporting them, each charterhouse must have been a local centre of feverish activity. There would be much building activity, either in wood or stone and tile. The

	Monastery	Dates occupied	Location
1	La Grande Chartreuse I	1084–1132	Dépt of Isère, France
2	La Grande Chartreuse II	1132 to present (with periods of abandonment)	
3	Rome ruined baths of Diocletian	1090	Rome, Italy
4	La Torre Santa Maria del Bosco I	1090–1192	Calabria, Italy
5	La Torre St Stephen II	1090–1192 (became Cistercian)	
6	Les Portes I	1115–1125	Dépt of Ain, France
7	Les Portes II	1125 to present (not continuously)	
8	St Sulpice en Bugey	1115/6 or 1123–1133 (became Cistercian)	Dépt of Ain, France
9	Meyriat	1116–1790	Dépt of Ain, France
10	Les Ecouges	1116–1294	Dépt of Isère, France
11	Durbon	1116–1178	Dépt of Hautes Alpes, France
12	La Sylve Benite	1116–1792	Dépt of Isère, France
13	Montrieux Le Vieux (1)	1117–1170	Dépt of Var, France
14	Montrieux Le Jeune (11)	1170–1792 (now re-occupied)	
15	Arvières I	1132–1142	Dépt of Ain, France
16	Arvières II	1142–1791	
17	Le Mont Dieu	1134–1793 (abandoned several times)	Dépt of Ardennes, France
18	'Aiaunus'	?1135? (transferred to Cistercian Buzay?)	
19	Vallon	1137/8–1544	Dépt of Haute Savoie, France
20	Vaucluse	1139–1901 (not continuously)	Dépt of Jura, France
21	Val St Pierre	1140/44–1791 (not continuously)	Dépt of Aisne, France

provision of firewood for cooking and keeping warm would be a constant activity, presumably with cycles of clearance and regeneration of woodland managed by the lay brethren. And of course food supplies, despite the sparse diet which was part of the community's regime, had to be procured. Much of this must have consisted of bread, vegetables, fruit and perhaps a little milk and cheese. If cattle and sheep were kept on these upland pastures, it would have been for wool for clothing and leather for footwear, rather than for meat, which was not allowed under the Rule.

Provision needed to be made for these commodities either from the landed estates of the charterhouse or from other local sources. The lower house must have acted as the monastic estate's farming centre as well as the home for the lay brethren. Rather like the Cistercians, the aim of the founders, and certainly of the Carthusians them-selves, was to acquire an area of land at the foundation of each house, so that they were not involved with lay people and farmers. No doubt this was not always achieved, but with a ring-fenced area the monks could determine the farming regime themselves with no involvement of communal farming or feudal obligations. On this land granges or outlying farms were built, run by lay brethren operating away from the correrie.

The lands around these early charterhouse sites in the Alps are peppered with 'grange' names. Of course, not all of these farms can be associated with the Carthusians: the Cistercians, and probably other monastic orders, were involved in farming the uplands as well, but some can be shown to have belonged to the local Carthusian house. An interesting early map of Les Portes Chartreuse and its land (7) survives with not only the monastery and the correrie depicted on it but also the granges of Coux, 2km to the south-east, and Ianvaix (now Janvais) 2km to the south. The boundary of the estate to the east is shown as the road from the villages of Arandas to Ordonnaz, 2 to 3km north-east of the monastery itself. The surrounding villages are shown in prospect and, even if the boundary between the lands of the villages and of the charterhouse ran only midway between them, this would still give the monastery an estate of approximately 5 by 7km (35km^2).

At La Grande Chartreuse we can get some idea of the use of the landscape around the monastery from the seventeenth-century prints. A prospect of 1670 viewed from the west shows the site of the original monastery (marked by Bruno's chapel and Notre Dame), the post-1132 monastery and the 'lower house' of 'La Courerie'. There are granges evident on the mountains around the site. Between the monastery and the correrie is St John's Grange, to the west on the Preries de Charrosette is the grange of Chartrouette, while to the south on another mountain massif in the Grandes Preries de Channanson is the grange of Charmonson. While these may have been the main establishments there are also at least two vaccaries, or cattle farms, and one bercary, a sheep farm, on the high ground. There are also a number of upland, probably summer pasture steadings on the mountains to the west and south of La Grande Chartreuse, to which we can imagine flocks and herds being taken once the snows had melted and the new spring growth of grass was coming through. At each of these there appears to be several small buildings for accommodation and processing. Even a rough guess would suggest that this estate was about 8-10km long and 5-6km wide (50km^2).

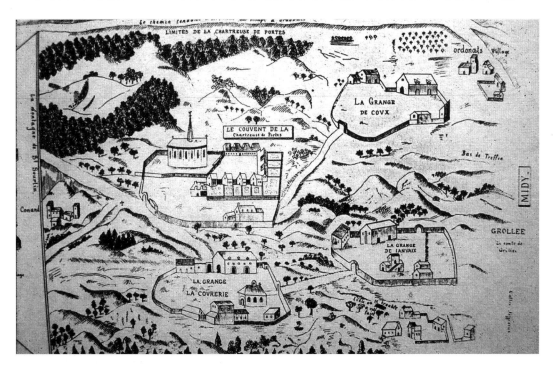

7 *An early map of the Les Portes area, with the correrie and outlying granges shown*

Expansion into Europe

The Carthusians arrived in Britain in 1178 with the establishment of Witham in Somerset. As the table above shows, by the end of Guigues' life and with the establishment of the communities in the Alps as a separately recognised 'order', charterhouses began to be built elsewhere in Europe. At first, a few were founded in the wooded hilly country of the Ardennes, in what is now northern France. By the end of the twelfth century, when they had established themselves successfully in England, there were altogether about 50 sites in Europe. Apart from the La Torre sites founded by Bruno in Calabria (Santa Maria and St Stephen), there were now other Italian sites in the Alps. Two had also been built in Slovenia, formerly part of Yugoslavia, and one in Spain, and Archbishop Eskild of Lund had attempted to introduce Carthusians into Scandinavia as part of his policy to bring the new orders to the Denmark. Otherwise the expansion had been principally in what is modern France, with a thin scatter across the centre and north of the country. It is, however, noticeable that most of the houses founded in the second half of the twelfth century were still in the region of the Alps (**8**).

Nevertheless by the time Witham was founded in Somerset in 1178, the main outlines of the first phase of the development of the Carthusian order sites were clear. The monks would require an isolated site, preferably in a 'desert', with no entanglements with existing feudal arrangements or peasant farmers to be dealt with. They would establish not only a main monastery for the hermit monks, the fathers, but

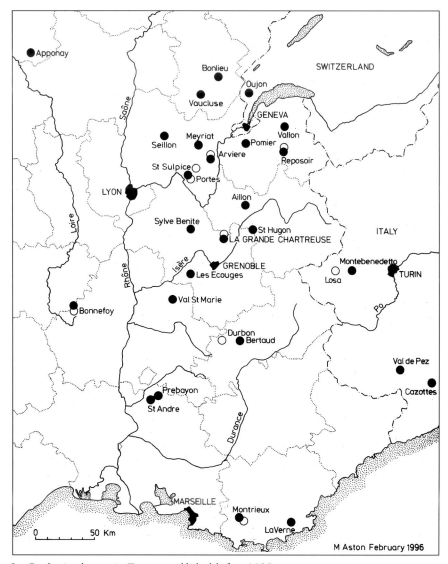

8 *Carthusian houses in Europe established before 1199*

also a lower house or correrie for the working monks – the brothers. Where possible granges, or outlying farms would be built to develop and exploit the land for the support of the community. It was to be a long time before the order which claimed to be 'never reformed because never deformed' was to change subtly, losing some of its lay brethren and lower houses and choosing sites which were much more in touch with humanity, in low-lying and even suburban locations, adjacent to all the major cities of medieval Europe.

2 The planning of Carthusian monasteries

Ever since the ninth century, the planning of monasteries about a square cloister, exemplified by the early ninth-century plan of an idealised monastery that survives in the library of the Swiss monastery at St Gall, had been common in Europe. The most important building, which normally occupied the north side of the cloister, was the church, and by the tenth century it was frequently cruciform in plan, with a nave, transepts, and presbytery which housed the main altar (**9**). The east side of the cloister comprised the communal dormitory at first floor level over the chapter house where daily business and discipline were addressed, the parlour where limited talking was allowed, and a work room for the community. The south range contained the refectory or dining hall and the kitchen, and the western side comprised storage and the outer parlour where members of the community could meet with the outside world. The

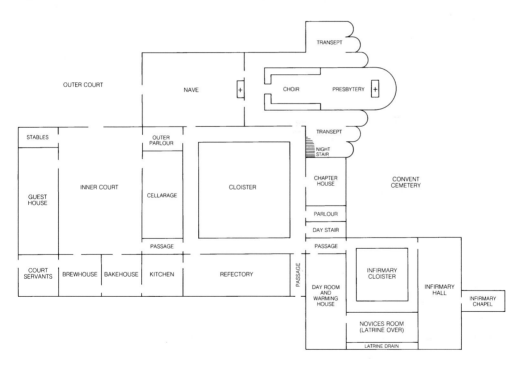

9 *A typical Benedictine or Cluniac plan of the late eleventh century*

upper floor was often reserved for the abbot or prior. Surrounding the central buildings were two service areas; the inner court with its guest accommodation, stabling, bake-house, brew-house and granaries, and the outer court with its animal houses, barns, and industrial buildings. This was the plan which monasteries in England had begun to adopt after St Ethelwold's *Regularis Concordia* of *c*.970 had introduced current Benedictine practice from the monastic reform that had swept through Germany and France. It was also the plan-form used by the new monasteries of the Benedictine and Cluniac orders founded by the Norman settlers after 1066. This, though, was the planning of monks who lived communal lives, who lived and prayed together.

The earliest Carthusian monasteries

The early Carthusians did not live communally. As Guibert of Nogent noted after a visit to the Grande Chartreuse in the early years of the twelfth century

> there were thirteen monks, having indeed a cloister sufficiently fit for communal life, but not living together in a cloister, for they all have cells of their own round the cloister, in which they work, sleep, and eat.

This was not a peculiarity of the Carthusians alone, for it was a practice shared with the monks of Camoldi and Vallambrosa in northern Italy, a development of the Egyptian communities of the fourth and fifth centuries. It was the Carthusians, however, who were to spread this idea across Europe in the first half of the twelfth century. Unfortunately, little more is known about the planning of early Carthusian monasteries, unlike those of the Cistercians, their brothers in reform. This is because their earliest buildings were largely of timber and have nowhere survived. There are hints provided by the *Customs* of Guigues de St-Romaine, fifth prior of the Grande Chartreuse which, written in about 1128 at the request of the priors of Portes, St-Sulpice, and Meyriat, is a document as critical to the Carthusians as Stephen Harding's *Exordium Parvum* (the *Little Introduction*) was to the Cistercians a decade earlier.

Prior Guigues identified for the first time that the Carthusians comprised two communities, the monks themselves who occupied the 'upper house' directed by the prior himself, and a 'lower house' managed by the procurator that housed the lay brethren. Both houses had churches which were to be simple, without gold and silver, carpets, or hangings. Monks were to be housed individually in 'cells' which did not initially have their own gardens, though an opportunity was provided for gardening outside the cloister. Unlike other orders, the Carthusians did not encourage guests, and if anyone did visit, they were to be housed with the lay brethren in the separate and detached 'lower house' unless they were monks or senior clergy. The monastery was only to accept sufficient land to support itself, and any surplus produce was to be given to religious communities who were poorer than the Carthusians. The prior was to deal with external affairs, and although important business was to be discussed with the community, no mention is made of a chapter house where business was conducted by other orders. Mature monks were to be given 'obediences', to run departments of the monastery such as the 'lower house' and the kitchen, very much as other orders managed their affairs, but there were fewer officers appointed because departments like the infirmary and guest house typical of communal orders did not exist in an early Carthusian context. Because the Carthusians had no need to communicate with each other, there did not need to be a parlour (although time was allowed for essential conversation in the cloister itself), and because their daily needs were provided within their cells, there was no reason for a day room or warming house to be provided. Meals were only taken together on Sundays, festivals, and on the day of the burial of a member of the community, so a refectory was provided, although it was small, and a cemetery was provided within the cloister garth which might only be used by members of the community or a monk of another order who had died in their house (but only if his own monastery could not carry his body away).

The 'lower house', so called because it was built lower down the mountain at the Grande Chartreuse, appears to have been more conventional in its planning. Lay brethren had a common dormitory and refectory where they were to eat in silence 'in the manner of the Cistercians'. It also contained the buildings found in the inner court of a regular monastery, the bake-house and granaries, and the cheese-house. There was also a garden. When the lay brethren were required to be in the 'upper house', they were to use the common dormitory provided for them there.

The charterhouse of Witham in Somerset

The development of a Carthusian plan was probably fairly rapid, for like the Cistercians they were remarkably single-minded, and new communities began with a core of experienced monks taken from existing monasteries. When the first house in England was established at Witham, it was the Grande Chartreuse that provided the founding party in 1178/9, led by a monk called Narbert. He took with him two lay brethren, Gerard, a very religious man, and Ainard, a centenarian who had been employed previously to set up new monasteries. Possibly there were others but they are not recorded. They would have taken with them the traditions of their own house, and had they succeeded would have established something very similar to the community they had left at the stage of development it had reached.

The foundation of Witham, by Henry I in his Royal Forest of Selwood in Somerset as a part of his penance for the murder of Archbishop Thomas Becket of Canterbury, tells us a great deal about early Carthusian life and aspirations because it went so badly wrong and had to be rescued. Initially, the King had approached the prior of the Grande Chartreuse offering a site in an area he controlled completely and which could be emptied of people to create the 'desert' the Carthusians desired. He did very little more, and a founding party was dispatched to colonise the site. The three men sent, though undoubtedly experienced, could not have been less suitable unless there was a total reliance on divine intervention. There probably was, though this was not a peculiarity of Christ's Poor Men. They found that the King had done little apart from removing his earlier tenant, and the local population proved troublesome. Henry had provided £10 for the 'brothers of the order of Chartuse dwelling in the vill of Witham which William FitzJohn had', but had done little else. Narbert could not cope and was recalled to France to be replaced by a new monk, Hamon, who fared little better and died shortly after his arrival from exposure. It was at this time that Henry I began to provide more seriously for the community, which must have been growing and building, providing £40 towards their work and £13 6s 8d (£13.33) for their clothing. He also requested a new prior from the Grande Chartreuse, and this time named his own choice. He asked for the procurator, Hugh of Avalon, a rising star among the Carthusians. Hugh arrived at Witham in 1180, and found the brothers living in timber cells enclosed within an earthen bank and palisade. The site of the new monastery had not even been laid out, and the displaced occupants of the vill of Witham had not yet been compensated for their loss. Hugh also discovered that the Augustinian priory of Bruton had an interest in the vill, including a chapel. Effectively, Hugh had to start the foundation afresh, convincing the King to resettle his tenants elsewhere and to replace Bruton Priory's interests with a church of like value. He also had to persuade Henry to find sufficient money for buildings. Only then could the serious business of setting up a new charterhouse begin.

Almost immediately after Hugh arrived, substantial payments began to appear in the royal accounts, taken from the forests of Sherwood and Chippenham, from the taxation of the counties of Somerset, Dorset, Devon, and Berkshire and from the abbeys of Glastonbury and Abingdon (temporarily in royal hands during abbatial vacancies). Money was provided for buildings, for the sustenance of the community, and for the white cloth used for their habits. By 1182, sufficient progress had been made for Henry to issue his official foundation charter. It would appear that the building work was actually commissioned by the King, for he paid two local men, Elyas de Massai and Walkelin of Bradley, to survey the site were the buildings were to be raised in 1181.

The lower house was centred on the chapel, or more probably parish church that Bruton Priory had established at Witham, which was retained for the lay brethren and survives as the church of Witham Friary. Curiously, the Carthusians removed the nave roof, thickened the walls, and installed a stone barrel vault very much in the French tradition, though they did little else. The village, however, was swept away and new timber buildings erected. To the west of the church was a kitchen built of wattles, and about 2m from that was the guest house, again a timber building with a roof of shingles. The location of other buildings is less well evidenced.

The site of the upper house today is represented by the earthworks of the great cloister and inner court, and an overlying post-medieval house and its gardens (**10**). In spite of its extensive remodelling to create garden terraces, the area of the great cloister can still be seen, measuring some 58 x 73m; excavation and geophysical survey have revealed that it had stone cells and gardens around it. There were also cloister alleys 3m wide. Our problem is that the stone buildings were not twelfth century in date, but represent a rebuilding from the early thirteenth century. The church can be located well to the north of the cloister. From the grants of money that Hugh received, it is fairly certain

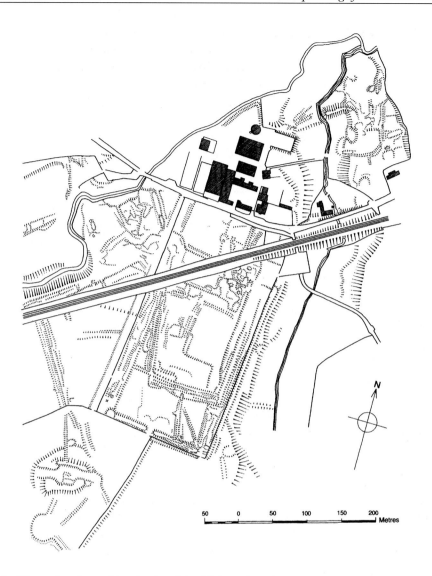

10 *The earthworks marking the site of the Witham charterhouse*

that he provided timber cells for his monks on the sites of their stone replacements. Only one stone building was recorded during Hugh's priorate and that was the church, the first payment for which was recorded in 1186/7. It is likely that this is the church which was still standing in the 1720s or 30s. If this is the case, a plan can be reconstructed featuring cells around a large rectangular cloister with a detached church some 60m to the north. As other orders placed the church on one side of their cloister this marks a substantial departure from the monastic norm, albeit one determined by an experienced monk of the Grande Chartreuse. We know from Adam of Eynsham's *Magna Vita Hugonis* (*Great Life of Hugh*) that the community comprised 20 to 30 men in Hugh's lifetime, which would suggest that Witham followed the Carthusian norm of a prior,

12 monks and 10 or more lay brethren, and that Hugh visited his old community every year after he became Bishop of Lincoln, keeping a close eye on how it was developing. What he laid out in the Forest of Selwood was a standard contemporary Carthusian charterhouse.

It took time to establish any monastery, and when Hugh left Witham it was still very much a temporary version, a form which was not peculiar to the Carthusians. Rebuilding would follow in stone as the creation of an estate and the building of an economy would allow. The site he had chosen, however, was a good one on a low ridge between the River Frome and an unnamed tributary, with an adequate provision of water and good drainage. Being placed in a Royal Forest ensured the necessary seclusion, so successfully in fact that Alexander of Lewes, a secular canon who had joined the community during Hugh's priorate, complained that he had been seduced into 'a horrible place, an empty solitude, inhabited only by wild animals', something that the reforming orders seem to have sought out as a matter of course. There was also scope for expansion and development, and this began in earnest in the first quarter of the thirteenth century. Two dams were built across the Frome (**10**) to enclose fishponds and the tributary was also dammed to serve a mill, both necessary to support monastic life and almost certainly planned from the time the monastery was laid out. The fishponds were certainly in place before 1323, when they are mentioned in a royal charter that granted the house woodland adjacent to them to increase the size of the priory's 'park' or enclosure. The first half of the thirteenth century was taken up with the provision of permanent buildings and the creation of an estate, evidenced by a flood of agreements with other religious houses who had an interest in the lands that Witham was acquiring in the vicinity. In this, Witham was behaving no differently to any other religious house, for there was very little land available in the twelfth and early thirteenth century in which someone else did not have an interest. As later Carthusian charterhouses were to find, it was a problem which became progressively more difficult to sort out as time progressed.

The charterhouse of Hinton in Somerset

Excavation at Witham in the late 1960s has done very little to establish the plan that was developed when permanent buildings were raised, and it is necessary to look elsewhere for the evidence for the planning of an early thirteenth-century charterhouse. In 1222, William Longespée, Earl of Salisbury and a bastard son of Henry II, established a second charterhouse at Hatherop, drawing the founding community from Witham and possibly from French houses. This new foundation did not suffer from the initial reluctance of the founder to discharge his obligations and William provided in his will of 1226 the profits of the wardship of his daughter-in-law until she reached her majority to fund their buildings, a gold chalice set with rubies and emeralds (something the monks should not have accepted), a pyx of gold set with pearls, two phials of silver, the finest set of vestments from his private chapel, and all his relics. He had clearly already provided temporary structures, and it was his

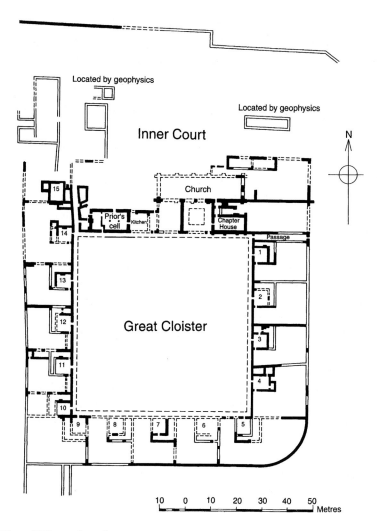

Inner Court

Located by geophysics

Located by geophysics

N

Church

Prior's cell

Kitchen

Chapter House

Passage

Great Cloister

15

14

13

12

11

10

9

8

7

6

5

4

3

2

1

10 0 10 20 30 40 50
Metres

11 *Plan of Hinton charterhouse*

intention that at his death they should commence their permanent buildings. For their further support he gave them 1000 ewes, 40 rams, 48 oxen, and 20 bulls. The location, however, was not to the monks liking because it did not afford the solitude they required, and on his death in 1226 they petitioned his countess, Ela, for a new site. The following year she gave them her manors of Hinton and Norton in exchange for their old site, and began the building of permanent buildings in her deer park at Hinton. The buildings were sufficiently complete to be consecrated in May 1232. Parts of this monastery survive, and excavation has revealed the greater part of its plan (**11**). So attractive was the site that the monks named it *Locus Dei* or God's Place, following a tradition which had been begun by the Cistercians in the very first decade of the twelfth century.

Like Witham, Hinton was divided into an upper and lower house. The lower house, or correrie can still be partially traced as earthworks about a mile to the east on the bank of the River Frome in the hamlet of Friary, and the upper house was placed on a substantial terrace above a north-south spur overlooking the Frome. Today, it is the site of a surviving late sixteenth-century house, its gardens, outbuildings, and what is known of its plan are the results of excavations by Major Philip Fletcher and his sons between 1950-9 with some further work in the 1960s, and a survey of the surviving earthworks and geophysical survey undertaken in 1995. Two medieval buildings actually survive; the prior's cell with the refectory above it, and the chapter house and a part of the church, both standing on the north side of the great cloister. All visible masonry dates to the second and third quarters of the thirteenth century (**colour plate 2**).

The plan of Hinton fixes the planning of a Carthusian charterhouse only a generation after Witham had been built in stone, and can be accepted as a typical layout following the norm set by continental houses of the order. There have been additions – for instance Cell 15 and a lengthening of the chapter house – but generally speaking there is every indication that the charterhouse remained more or less as first built until it was suppressed in 1538. Like all English monasteries it was divided into three enclosures, the cloister, inner court, and outer court (which in this case was the correrie or lower house). The cloister was $70m^2$, with cells and their gardens along the west, south, and east sides. The north side comprised the prior's cell, refectory, kitchen, and chapter house. A narrow cloister alley ran around all four sides of the great cloister, not the wide cloister typical of the greater monasteries which served as the monks' living room and work place, but little more than a covered corridor that connected the cells with the church and common offices of the north range. The garth of the great cloister was a garden, and geophysical survey has located gravel paths dividing it into four equal plots. One, probably that in the north-east corner, comprised the convent cemetery.

The church lay to the north of the great cloister as at Witham, but here was connected to it by a lesser cloister or court enclosed with galleries. This form of communication is common in later charterhouses and may have existed at Witham. Attached to the east end of the church was a two-roomed cell and garden, almost certainly for the sacrist who was responsible for the care of the church and chapter house.

To the north of the church and the north range of the great cloister was the inner court, enclosed by a wall and originally entered by a gate house, though this has not been traced. Its buildings are only known from geophysical survey, but would have comprised service buildings like the brew-house and bake-house and the granaries that served them. From the inner court was the entrance into the north-west corner of the great cloister, conveniently close to the prior's cell so that access could easily be controlled. Strangely, a second entrance was placed at the north-east corner of the great cloister, indicating that the inner court must have continued along the east side of the gardens there. The inner court was normally a semi-public area. Other orders placed their guest houses and stables there, but the Carthusians placed guests and stables in the correrie, and the nature of Carthusian inner courts before the late fourteenth century remains almost unknown.

The second phase of Carthusian expansion in England and the charterhouse of Beauvale in Nottinghamshire

With the foundation of Witham, the Carthusian expansion into England came to a halt. There were two reasons for this; the reluctance of monks to choose such an austere life when they could join the Cistercians or smaller strict orders like the Grandmontines and enjoy a communal life, and the fact that monastic life seemed less relevant after the arrival of the Franciscan friars in the 1220s. Another factor was the reluctance among landowners to part with sufficient land to endow a charterhouse, particularly when the friars made it clear that they did not want land, only alms. Monastic foundations tailed off dramatically from the early years of the thirteenth century, and the Carthusians were rather unlucky in their timing. Interest in the order was, however, reawakened in the second quarter of the fourteenth century. The prior of the Grande Chartreuse and the general chapter of the order asked Edward I if he could facilitate the foundation of a third house in his kingdom in the early 1270s; the request was granted, but not in England. The result was the foundation of an Irish house at Kinaleghin in County Galway which survived only until 1308.

In 1331, Edward III licensed the creation of a charterhouse in Exeter, but nothing came of this. It does, however, indicate the resurgence of interest in the order which was becoming apparent across Europe. In 1343, Sir Nicolas de Cantilupe, lord of Greasley and a courtier and soldier, established a charterhouse at Beauvale on his demesnes in Nottinghamshire. He approached the prior of Hinton, which was to provide the founding community, and as at Hinton, the monastery was built in his deer-park. The naming tradition was also brought from God's Place at Hinton; the community called their new site *Pulchra Vallis*, Beauvale in Norman French, or the Beautiful Valley in English. The foundation charter gives a clear indication of why the monastery was founded and of Cantilupe's connections: the monks were to pray for his lord King Edward III, his cousin William Zouch, Archbishop of York, and Lord Henry of Lancaster, earl of Derby and for Cantilupe himself, his son, his wife Joan, and the soul of his first wife Tiphany. He was creating a mausoleum for himself and associating his patrons with it.

The site, on the edge of Sherwood Forest, had all the advantages and disadvantages that the royal forest of Selwood had provided for Witham. The charterhouse was built on the side of a south facing wooded hill on an artificial terrace, and is still marked by the ruins of the church and an adjacent building and substantial earthworks. The site was excavated in 1908 by the Rev de Boulay Hill and Harry Gill for the Thoroton Society of Nottingham, and the greater part of its plan recovered. The earthworks were surveyed and the site geophysically surveyed in 1995, providing additional detail. Where Witham and Hinton had been laid out with a north-south axis, the hillside site at Beauvale required the axis to lie east-west, with the great cloister lying to the west of the church and inner court (**12**). The great cloister measured 58m x 56m and had the same narrow cloister alleys as Hinton, with 14 cells and gardens on its north, west, and south sides. The east side of the great cloister is

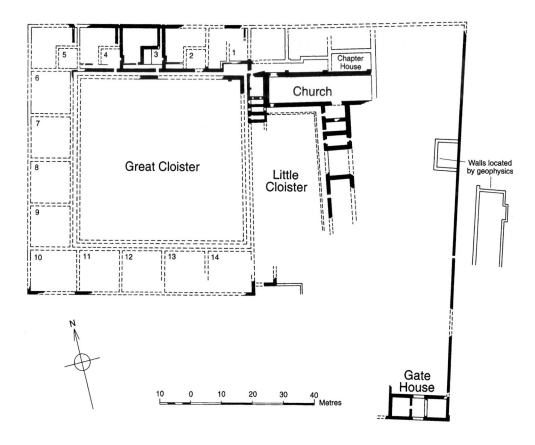

12 *Plan of Beauvale charterhouse*

partly buried below later farm buildings, but must have contained the prior's cell, refectory, and kitchen.

The general disposition of buildings is the same as at Hinton, but there are signs of development. How much of this is a result of later rebuilding will remain uncertain until there has been modern excavation. The church and the building at its south-west corner, however, do appear to be early fourteenth-century buildings and Nicholas de Cantilupe claimed to have built the church and cells within three years of the foundation (**colour plate 3**). Such timing would suggest that only key buildings such as the church, prior's cell, and refectory were initially built in stone, and though the site was fully laid out, most of the other buildings would have been of timber in the position of their stone successors. The church was separated from the great cloister by a small yard, but was not entered from it. Instead, a passage through the east range led to a door at the west end of the south wall, and a continuation of the north alley of the great cloister led to a larger door in the north wall which was probably the main entrance for the monks. A little cloister was provided on the south side of the church but this was a secondary feature, and the inner court lay to the east of this, bounded by a wall, and with a surviving gatehouse at the south-east corner. The disposition of the inner court remains largely unknown. One building has been located on its east side, but equally important, a second building has been located outside the boundary wall.

What complicates the situation at Beauvale is the fact that there is no reference to a lower house or correrie and it is by no means certain whether the lay brethren were housed separately or within the upper house. This is of the greatest significance, for the fourteenth century saw a change in the planning of English and many European charterhouses as the lay brethren were brought inside the main enclosure. This would have required a degree of re-planning which might indicate why the little cloister had become much bigger than that at Hinton, and it was been suggested by the excavators that the long building on the east side of the little cloister was, at its southern end, a communal dormitory for the lay brethren. The lack of a separate correrie meant that the offices of the outer court, the agricultural and industrial complex that supported monastic life, had to be accommodated within the confines of the upper house, and the earthworks at Beauvale clearly indicate that the enclosure of the great cloister and inner court lie inside a greater enclosure (**13**) with substantial building

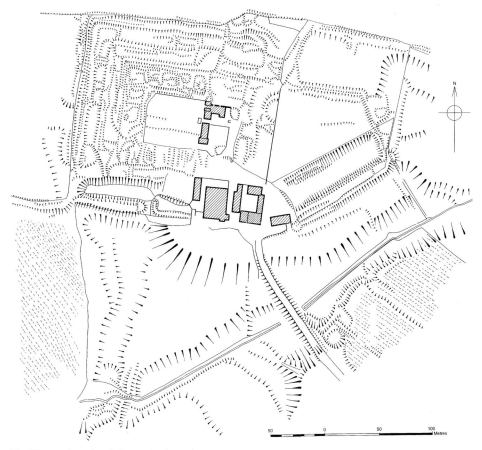

13 *The earthworks of Beauvale charterhouse*

platforms, access routes, and water courses. There is even a separate access causeway from the east into the outer court, implying that it had its own gatehouse. Essentially, a Carthusian charterhouse now resembled in its overall planning the monasteries of other orders in England.

One other change can be detected at Beauvale. The chapter house, not a building of the primary phase, was placed against the north side of the church where it could be entered directly from the monks' choir. At Hinton, the church and chapter house were separated by a passage and a sacristy, an approach which was abandoned before the late fourteenth century but which had always been rare in continental houses of the order. Perhaps this was a return to a European model and a move away from something which had developed in Cistercian churches and been adopted by the Carthusians of Hinton. Whatever the reason, all later Carthusian chapter houses in England were built directly against the church and were not directly accessible from the great cloister.

The Black Death and the foundation of the London charterhouse

The renewed interest in the Carthusian order is further underlined by the projected foundation of another house at Horne in Surrey in about 1345. It does not seem to have been carried forward, and apart from a royal licence nothing further is known of this attempt. It may well be that it foundered with many other projects when England was ravaged by the Black Death in 1348-9.

It was not only the reduction in the population by between a quarter and a half that affected religious houses; it was the crisis in confidence it engendered that led to a renewed interest in the stricter forms of monasticism. Sudden and disfiguring death had to be the result of serious omissions in religious fervour, and two religious groups were to benefit. The first was the friars whose houses in towns had put them at the centre of care for the sick and the disposal of their bodies; the second was the Carthusians, whose strict and unassuming life was believed to make their prayers and masses all the more powerful. A recurrence of the plague in 1360-4 only served to strengthen this move, and the result was a crop of new charterhouses, not only in England but across Europe. It was in this phase that the great charterhouses of Miraflores in Spain, Champmol in Burgundy, and Pavia in northern Italy were established as indications of royal and national piety.

In 1371 Sir Walter Maney, a courtier, soldier, and personal friend of Edward III who professed a 'special devotion' to the Carthusian order established a charterhouse outside the walls of London in Smithfield, on a plot of land that he had acquired in 1349 for use as a plague cemetery and on which he built a chapel and eventually a hermitage. At the time, he was not at all sure what he wanted to do with the site, and although he had introduced two hermits, he also sought a papal licence to build a college of 12 priests who would say masses for the dead. He was finally persuaded by the Bishop of London, Michael de Northburgh, who had recently stayed in the charterhouse of Paris to establish a charterhouse on the site, which he would help to endow. This was far from easy. The priors of both Witham and Hinton were

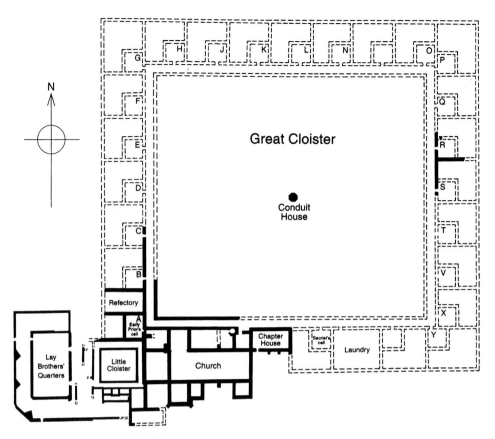

Great Cloister

Conduit
House

Refectory

Early
Prior's
cell

Lay
Brothers'
Quarters

Little
Cloister

Church

Chapter
House

Sacrist's
cell

Laundry

14 *Plan of the London charterhouse*

consulted but both died before any conclusion could be reached, and then John Luscote, the new prior of Hinton, was reluctant to establish a house in a place which was unsuitable for Carthusian life. However, Maney was convinced that he should proceed and persuaded the prior of the Grande Chartreuse to support the new foundation. In 1371, John Luscote was appointed prior, two monks were detached from Witham, two monks and a lay brother were sent from Hinton, a further two monks came from Beauvale and the new monastery was established. From the date of its foundation it was to be known as the House of the Salutation of the Mother of God. In line with the heightened religious observance of the time, an overtly religious name was chosen for the community, a practice which was followed into the early fifteenth century. Henry Yevely, master of the King's Works, was commissioned to lay out the cloister and build the first cell.

The plan of the London charterhouse is known from three sources (**14**); a plan drawn in the 1430s, excavation by W.F. Grimes in 1948-9 and 1959, and surviving buildings within a post-suppression house. Where charterhouses normally comprised twelve monks and a prior, London was a double house of 24, much larger than any of the houses in England that preceded it. At its centre was a great cloister 51 x 44m, initially with cells on the west, north, and east sides, each with a walled garden. The church lay to the south of the great cloister, separated by an enclosed yard or garden, but was joined to the south cloister alley by a low tower which still exists. The lesser cloister lay to the west of the church, though in the form of a later rebuilding, and to its west was accommodation for the lay brethren The chapter house lay immediately to the east of the church and was connected to it by the low tower. It, too, survives within the post-medieval house which was built on the site of the church. Exceptionally, the prior's cell (Cell A) and the refectory were placed in the west alley of the great cloister. As the charterhouse developed, its cells were to continue on the south side of the cloister, each identified by a letter on the 1430s plan. The south-west quadrant of the great cloister was used as the convent cemetery, and is the only one in England that has ever been examined archaeologically.

The inner court, which contained guest accommodation, the meat kitchen, and meat refectory lay to the south of the church, and although these buildings are known from documents they neither appear on the 1430s plan, nor were traced by excavation. Because the London charterhouse was built on a cramped site hemmed in with other buildings, there was no space for an outer court, and the face the house presented to the outside world was the gate of the inner court that still survives today.

The charterhouses of Hull, Coventry, and Axholme

The building of the London charterhouse brought the Carthusians to the attention of the world at large, and a flurry of new foundations followed. The first was at Hull, where Sir William de la Pole was considering the foundation of a hospital of chaplains and poor people in 1365. He later changed his mind and sought to replace the intended chaplains with Franciscan nuns, and though he had started building he died before he could fully put his ideas into effect. It was left to his son Michael de la Pole, later the first earl of Suffolk, to fulfil his wishes, and he chose Carthusian monks. Like Walter Maney and Nicholas de Cantilupe before him, Michael de la Pole was a prominent courtier and soldier, a protégé of John of Gaunt, and in December 1377 he was made personal advisor to the young Richard II when Gaunt became King of Castile. Support for the Carthusians was a feature of most of the royal courts of Europe, and it comes as no surprise that de la Pole chose the order to occupy the new foundation at Hull. In 1389, the house of St Michael the Archangel was formally established in Hull on the site of the Maison Dieu, his father's hospital, outside the north gate of the walled town. Nothing is known of the plan of this monastery which was intended for a community of 13, though documents make it clear both that the hospital survived alongside the charterhouse though under separate management, and that after the suppression, the name of the charterhouse was transferred to the hospital.

The foundation of the charterhouse of Coventry was less well-organised than that at Hull, but perhaps indicates how such foundations came to be made, as well as the slow progress in getting started. William, Lord Zouch of Harringworth, was

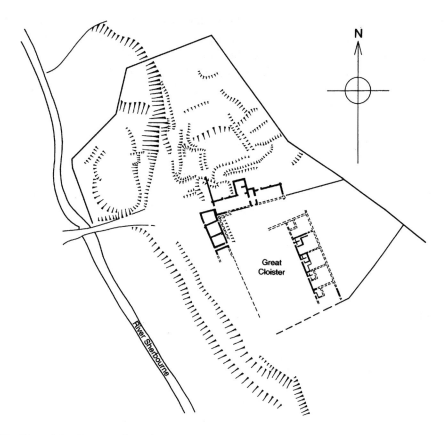

15 *Plan of the Coventry charterhouse*

approached by Robert Palmer, the procurator of the London house, to establish a charterhouse at Coventry, of which Palmer was to be the first prior. Two further monks from London and three from Beauvale were dispatched to become the founding community in 1375. They soon acquired four newly professed monks locally. William Zouch was to stand surety for the community and persuade Richard II to supply a site in the manor of Shortley outside the town, land he had to acquire. This was not accomplished until 1382, and the community took up residence in the former hermitage of St Anne. Zouch died in April 1382, but support was taken up by the burgesses of Coventry and by Richard II himself. Between 1382-5, construction of the first seven cells around a great cloister began, and in 1385, work started on a permanent church. Although this was stone-built it would appear that the cells, which each cost £20 to endow, must have been of timber. Parts of the church, the west range of the cloister and a substantial part of the enclosing precinct wall are still standing, and the church and east range of the cloister were excavated by Coventry Museums between 1968 and 1987 (**15**). Additionally, the earthworks of the precinct have been surveyed and limited geophysical survey carried out. Only a partial plan has been recovered.

St Anne's charterhouse, named after both the hermitage that had provided the first home for the community and the patron saint of Richard II's wife, was built on a raised terrace on the east side of the River Sherbourne, and bounded by a precinct wall about 3m high that survives on the west, north, and east sides. Centrally placed within this boundary was the rectangular great cloister 42 x 65m, with cells placed around its east, south, and west sides. It was not aligned north-south but was more or less parallel to the river. The church lay to the north, separated from the cloister by a wedge-shaped court that was bounded on its west side by the surviving prior's cell and refectory. This last building butted against the south-west angle of the church and had a gallery along its inner side that returned along the south wall of the church. Excavation has revealed slight traces of buildings to the north of the church that the excavators have identified as the little cloister. Earthworks indicating building platforms would suggest that this interpretation is correct, and that the enclosed court between the refectory and church is an enclosure similar to that separating the church from the great cloister at Beauvale. Coventry charterhouse had to provide accommodation around its little cloister for the lay brethren, though it is uncertain whether this was in the form of communal buildings, or the individual cells which appear in later houses. Access to the monastery was from the west on a causeway across the floodplain of the Sherbourne, and this entered the precinct to the west of the church, suggesting that this was the access to the church and inner court. Entry to the great cloister was a narrow passage in the west range immediately to the south of the prior's cell, where he could control the seclusion of the enclosure.

A third charterhouse belongs to this group, that of Axholme or Epworth in Lincolnshire. Thomas Mowbray, Earl of Nottingham, had originally intended to convert the alien priory of Monks Kirby in Warwickshire to a charterhouse. Monks Kirby had been founded and endowed by his family and given to the Benedictine abbey of St Nicholas at Angers. It only had two monks, and because England was at war with France it might be taken back and put to another suitable religious use; and so Mowbray acquired a papal licence in 1389 to refound it as a Carthusian monastery. For some reason, this did not happen and Mowbray turned his attention to another site. At Low Melwood in the Isle of Axholme, a part of Mowbray's manor of Epworth was a chapel that had been served by a college of priests since the late twelfth century. By the 1370s it had apparently gone out of use. It was not until 1397/8 that Mowbray actually got round to establishing his new monastery, despite the fact that he had been given royal licence, and John de Moreby appointed prior, in 1395. The new house took the name of the House of the Visitation of the Blessed Virgin Mary.

Axholme charterhouse can still be traced as a fine series of earthworks at Low Melwood Farm on the gravel terrace above the River Trent (**16**). There has been a small amount of excavation (by the late Peter Wenham in 1968), and the earthworks were plotted and a geophysical survey carried out in 1995. The situation is complicated by two factors: the church was the chapel of a pre-existing religious community modified and extended to suit the Carthusians; and the site was occupied by two major post-medieval houses with extensive gardens that have

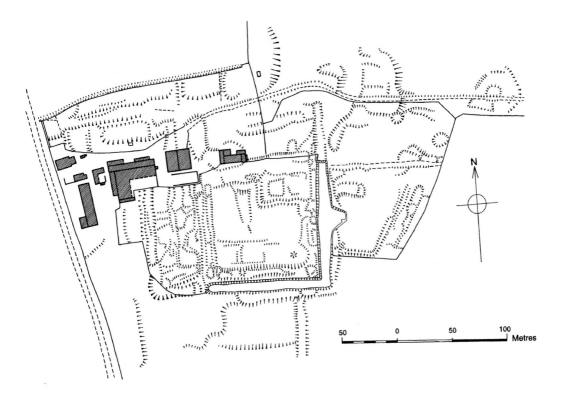

16 *The earthworks of Axholme charterhouse*

substantially modified the layout. However, geophysical survey has identified both the cells on the west, south, and east sides of the great cloister, and the location of the post-medieval houses that occupied the north side. The 'moat' which defines the south and west sides is in fact a post-suppression garden feature, and its dry western arm lies within the great cloister immediately to the east of the western range of cells. The great cloister itself was 70m², with narrow alleys which can still be traced on the south and east sides, and the farmhouse which lies on top of the north range contains a vaulted cellar of fifteenth-century date which is a part of the charterhouse. The church must have been to the north of the north range and east of the farmhouse, but its site cannot be identified. To the north of the farm buildings is the medieval entrance to the site, presumably heading in the direction of the inner court and church. The earthworks on the eastern side of the site, which are not aligned on the north-south cloister ranges, most probably represent the outer court of the monastery.

Hull, Coventry, and Axholme were all founded by members of the royal court, and Richard II had also involved himself in the foundation of Coventry, naming himself as patron. These foundations however were all reasonably modest; the next and final two were to be royal foundations of much greater scale.

The charterhouse of Mount Grace

Thomas de Holand, earl of Kent and duke of Surrey, Earl Marshall of England and Governor of Ireland, was the son of Richard II's half-brother and a royal favourite. On inheriting his father's estates in 1397 he decided within a year to establish a charterhouse to mark his special devotion and 'very strong affection' for the Carthusian order. His brother-in-law, Gian Galeazzo Visconti had similarly established the charterhouse of Pavia, and it was as much a mark of his status as his devotion. The site chosen was the manor of Bordelby on the western edge of the North Yorkshire Moors, not land that de Holand actually owned. It belonged to Thomas de Ingleby, who was associated with the foundation but who lacked the resources to establish a monastery himself. Endowment came from a clutch of alien priories recently seized because of the war with France, and bought from Richard II. The new house had two names: the House of Mount Grace of Ingelby, which served for everyday use; and the more formal House of the Assumption of the Blessed Virgin and of St Nicholas, commemorating feasts that were especially important to the founder. Thomas de Holand barely survived the deposition of his uncle in 1399 and rose in revolt against Henry IV, dying at Cirencester in 1400. A new patron of similar status, Thomas Beaufort, earl of Dorset and later duke of Exeter, uncle to Henry V, saw the completion of the greater part of the monastery and the expansion of its community. As with Axholme, the source of the founding community is not known, but given later evidence some at least must have come from the London charterhouse.

Mount Grace is the best preserved of the English houses of the order (**17**), with substantial remains of the great cloister, church, and inner court, and excavation since 1898 and more particularly between 1957-92 has revealed most of the plan of the great and lesser cloisters and the inner court. The earthworks of the outer court were surveyed in 1995. The most important aspect of this work is in how it reveals the way in which the plan developed. Some of the assumptions made about earlier foundations are conditioned by what is known of Mount Grace. What is significant is that Mount Grace has produced evidence for four phases of development: a stone and timber first phase, a rebuilding in stone in the 1420s once the house had reached a stability equated with the patronage of Thomas Beaufort, an expansion in the 1470s reflecting the patronage of Edward IV, and a final phase dating to the 1520s that denotes its ultimate extent.

The site chosen for Mount Grace was a natural terrace formed by a post-glacial earth-slip at the base of the Cleveland escarpment (**colour plate 4**), an area with copious springs and small streams but no river. At the foundation, the terrace was levelled and extended to provide an area on which a great cloister could be built, not rectangular or square in form but trapezoidal, following the line of rising ground to the east. Only the south side of the cloister was built in stone; from west to east it comprised the prior's cell, the refectory, an open court (later filled with buildings), and the sacrist's cell. To the west of the prior's cell was a detached stone kitchen. Seven timber cells in ditched enclosures were built on the east and north sides of the

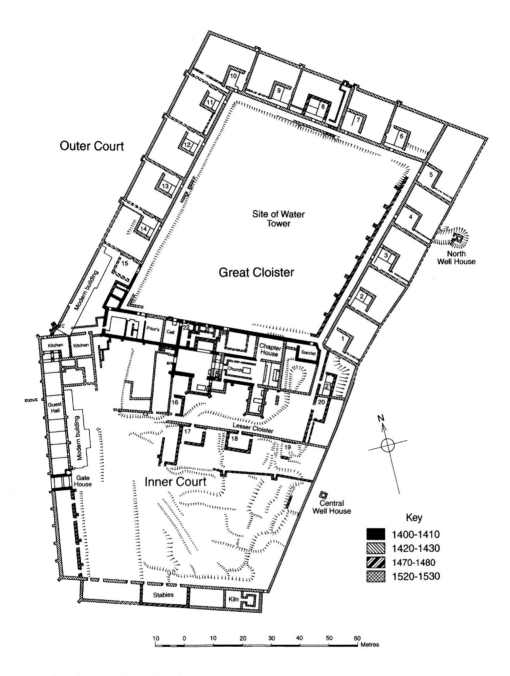

Outer Court

Great Cloister

Site of Water
Tower

North
Well House

Prior's Cell

Chapter
House

Sacrist

Church

Lesser Cloister

Inner Court

Kitchen

Kitchen

Guest
Hall

Gate
House

Modern building

Modern building

Stables

Kiln

Central
Well House

N

Key
1400-1410
1420-1430
1470-1480
1520-1530

10 0   10   20   30   40   50   60
                                    Metres

17 *Plan of Mount Grace charterhouse*

great cloister and the enclosure of an eighth was begun but never completed, and a cloister was built, also from wood, to serve these cells. On a lower terrace to the south of the south range was the church, its north wall aligned with the south wall of the refectory and prior's cell, separated from the cloister by the open court. To the south of the church, an inner court was enclosed, its only stone building being the gatehouse at its entrance. The buildings of the inner court, if they existed, must have been of timber. All of this had been achieved by 1412 when building ceased and the community petitioned Henry IV for support, saying that there were only nine men in the monastery and since the death of their founder they had had no support. There appear to have been no lay brethren at this stage. Effectively, Mount Grace had not achieved stability and was surviving in largely temporary buildings, though it had already established the scale and layout of its final buildings. The great cloister had been set out 70m wide by 65-81m deep. Thomas Beaufort's support enabled the community to complete its buildings, ultimately 15 cells and gardens around the great cloister, and five timber cells (later rebuilt as six stone cells) for lay brethren around a lesser cloister to the east and south of the church – the earliest known example of individual cells being built for lay brethren. Another departure was the building of a substantial guest house on the west side of the inner court, perhaps an indication that although guests were not supposed to be encouraged the popularity of the Carthusians drew visitors to their monasteries – and they did provide a useful source of income. Indeed the placing of the charterhouse on the road from York to Durham with its regular groups of pilgrims travelling to St Cuthbert's shrine may well have been intentional. A second guest dormitory had to be provided in the later fifteenth century.

The outer court lay on a third terrace to the west of the great cloister and inner court, and appears not to have been enclosed. It was apparently created in the 1420s when a watercourse was brought from two miles to the south to feed a mill, parts of which still survive. It has no fewer than three fishponds and a complicated series of water channels that augmented the house's meagre local water supply. Further west still was the home grange, the farm from which the local estates were managed, again with at least one surviving building of fifteenth-century date. The later history of Mount Grace is one of slow expansion, with additional cells being added to the great cloister, an indication of the appeal of Carthusian life in the later Middle Ages. In the 1520s, the charterhouse had a waiting list of four for the one available cell.

Mount Grace is the most developed of the English charterhouses, and its well-preserved buildings show a maturity of plan that was closely related to the London site. Because the plan of Hull is not known, the plan of Axholme only barely understood, and that of Coventry incomplete, London and Mount Grace stand out as the type-sites of the order in later medieval England. That they were so similar suggests that planning was tightly controlled and only slight variation was permitted. They do, however, present a remarkable advance on the plan of Hinton, the lone source of evidence for early thirteenth-century planning in England. It is particularly unfortunate that so little is known of the last and greatest of the English charterhouses.

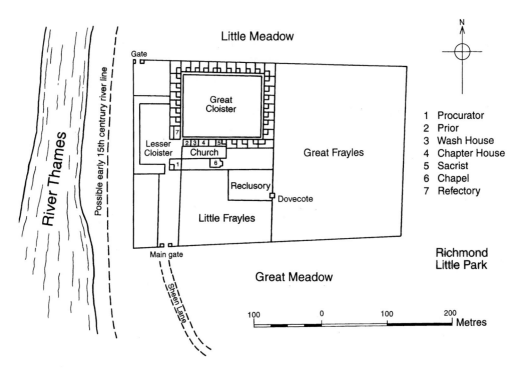

18 *Reconstructed plan of Sheen charterhouse*

The charterhouse of Sheen

The culmination of Carthusian development in England was the foundation of a charterhouse immediately to the north of the royal palace of Sheen (later renamed Richmond by Henry VII) in 1414 by Henry V. While Richard II's foundation of Coventry had been merely by adoption, this was an indication of royal piety comparable with Philip II of Spain's building of the palace monastery of the Escorial. It was to be called the House of Jesus of Bethlehem of Sheen, a further mark of its intended pre-eminence. Today it lies below the Royal Mid-Surrey Golf Course and is known only from parchmarks in the grass, a description by William of Worcester in the 1460s or 70s, and a Parliamentary survey of 1649 that describes the buildings which survived until after the Civil War.

Built in the palace park it was approximately twice the size of most charterhouses in England, having cells for a prior and 30 monks. The whole of the precinct (**18**) was enclosed by a brick wall and divided into two parts, the great and lesser cloisters and inner court (Little Frayles) to the west and the outer court (Great Frayles) to the east. The great cloister measured 120 x 90m, with cells on the east, north, and west sides, with the refectory at the south end of the west range, almost in the same position as the London charterhouse. The south range comprised the prior's cell, a wash house, the chapter house, the sacrist's cell, and four monks' cells, and the church lay directly south of the first four of these and was entered from the cloister through a small court between the chapter house and sacrist's cell. The lesser or little cloister lay to the west of the church and west range and housed the lay brethren and guests, with the procu-rator's cell being placed at the south-west angle of the church to control access to the enclosure. Within the inner court, a further enclosure was constructed.

Not content with founding a major charterhouse, Henry V required that provision be made for a building to house a recluse chaplain who might have even more time for prayer and contemplation than the choir monks. This chaplain, who was fed and clothed by the community, had his own garden and was sole occupant of what almost functioned as a monastery within a monastery.

Although Sheen charterhouse was suppressed in 1539 during the general dissolu-tion of the monasteries it was the only Carthusian monastery to be refounded by Mary I in 1555, its buildings surviving well enough to be restored to their former use. It was finally closed by Elizabeth I in 1559, upon which the small community moved to the charterhouse of Val de Grace at Bruges in Belgium.

3 Carthusian churches and chapter houses

In most monasteries, the church was the largest and most important building; because it was used for the seven daily offices and for Mass, it was literally the centre of religious life. For the Carthusians however it was the cell that was important, and the church was only used for the night office of Matins, for Vespers, and for Mass which was only celebrated on Sundays and festival days. The offices of Prime, Terce, Sext, None, and Compline were said privately in the cell oratory. In consequence, the Carthusians' churches were small and detached from the great cloister where the cells were placed. Because Carthusian communities were small, unlike the large communities of Benedictine or Cistercian houses, and because they did not have elaborate processions, Carthusian churches were more in keeping with the scale of parish churches than cathedrals. Up to the middle of the fourteenth century, separate churches were provided for the choir monks in the upper house and for the lay brethren in the lower house or correrie.

Early churches at Witham and Hinton

Very little is known of the first Carthusian church to be built in England at Witham. It was built in 1180-2, apparently of timber, and replaced by a new stone church begun in 1186/7 and still incomplete in 1190. The *Metrical Life of St Hugh*, who was the prior responsible for its construction, states that this was a stone building with bases and columns as if it had aisles. This church actually survived until 1762, incorporated in the post-medieval house of 1717. A description of the mansion built on the site after the suppression, probably in the early 1720s, tells us that this

> house is mostly new built & forms a quadrangle but the Old Dark Vaulted Carthusian Chapell is on the N side & now [a] Convenient Cellar, but the Pillars and Niches for Images and Holy Water plainly discover what it hath been but Instead of it there is a more light and Beautiful Chapell built which forms the south Side of the Quadrangle.

This description is close to that of the early thirteenth century given in St Hugh's life, although with the added information that the building was vaulted.

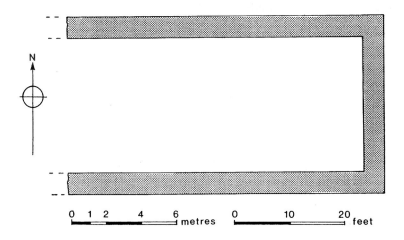

N

0 1 2 4   6 metres   0   10   20 feet

19 *Plan of the church at Witham*

Remarkably, its layout can be recovered from a plan of the house published in 1771 in Colen Cambell's *Vitruvius Britannicus* (**19**). Though the plan is drawn at first floor level, the walls of the north wing at 1.2m deep are shown to be considerably thicker than other parts of the house. They are in fact the upper parts of the church, that had been truncated at its west end when the house was built. It was a simple rectangular structure 7.65m wide internally and survived to a length of 17.3m. There is no indication whatsoever that the building was ever aisled, and the pillars of the description are almost certainly the wall-shafts that supported the springings of the vault and divided the building into bays. The east end was square and did not finish in an apse – this omission was an English affectation derived from the churches of the Augustinian canons and Cistercians rather than from European Carthusian models. In continental houses, the Carthusians normally favoured the apse.

The monks' church needs to be compared with the extant church of the lower house. Here, the church, which has an unaisled nave (the added aisle dates from the nineteenth century) and apsed chancel, actually predated the foundation of the charterhouse, but was modified to serve the lower house. Its planning, that of a parish church or chapel, probably owes more to the needs of Bruton Priory which built it than the aspirations of the Carthusians.

The church at Hinton (**20**), of which a fragment of the south wall survives, is known otherwise from Major Fletcher's excavation. As that work consisted of trenching to find walls and the high altar, nothing is known of its internal arrangements, and as the walls are largely reduced to footings, the position of only one surviving door is known. Like Witham it is rectangular in plan and was vaulted in five bays, measuring 28 x 7.9m with walls 1.2m thick. Though a generation later than St Hugh's church at Witham, there could well be a family resemblance. It was a tall and graceful building, rubble-built but with fine ashlar detailing, lit by twin lancet windows in each bay of its side walls. As seems to be the case at Witham, the vault is carried on triple wall-shafts that rise from a corbel below a moulded string-course at the level of the internal cills of the windows 2.5m above floor level. Something of the planning of this church can be reconstructed from the evidence that survives. Because the sacrist's cell lay to the north of the church, there must have been a door opposite that to the chapter house in the second bay from the east of the south wall and the monks' stalls must have been placed to the west of these doors, occupying the central bay of the church as there is no space to the east. The height of their stalls, which must have been without canopies, is dictated by the height of the stringcourse. Their quire was closed to the west by a screen, presumably at the junction between the third and fourth bays from the east, and this would place the monks' entrance into the church from the little cloister at the centre of the fourth bay from the east.

The church of God's Place at Hinton is particularly important because it appears to have remained in its original form throughout the life of the charterhouse, and provides a clear example of how English Carthusian churches were planned in the first half of the thirteenth century.

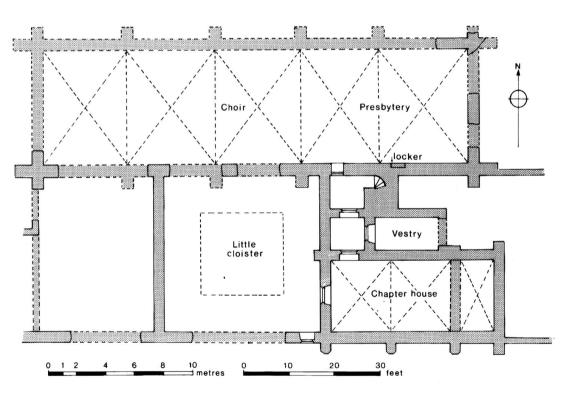

20 *Plan of the church and chapter house at Hinton*

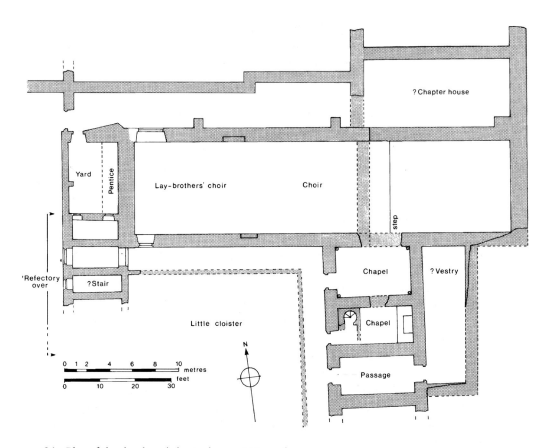

21 *Plan of the church and chapter house at Beauvale*

The church at Beauvale

If Witham and Hinton provide detail for late twelfth- and thirteenth-century churches of the order in England, the partially surviving church at Beauvale demonstrates how planning had developed by the early fourteenth century. In particular, there were new models to follow, especially the churches of the friars which had stripped out the excesses (as they saw them) of other monastic orders. Remarkably, the church that Nicholas de Cantelupe raised at Beauvale in 1343-6 had a great deal in common with the two earlier churches (**21**). It was a plain rectangular building measuring 20.4 x 8.2m, entered not centrally, but at the west end of its side walls. Originally without buttresses, it appears to have been of four bays, but unlike the earlier churches it did not have a vault. No trace remains of the original windows in its rubble walling; they must have been set high in the walls as they were at Hinton **(colour plate 3)**. Its western bay was little more than a porch, but otherwise the planning seems to have followed that at Hinton (which was a bay longer).

The significance of the church at Beauvale is that it was altered within a generation of its being built, indicating that the community's needs were developing. If this only related to Beauvale it might be the result of extending an inadequate church which had been provided to meet the immediate needs of foundation – but it does not. All later churches, where the evidence can be recovered, show similar evidence of expansion.

The east wall of the original church was taken down and the building extended by 13.4m, while the windows were replaced by large traceried styles, one of which survives in the south wall at its west end. Buttresses were added to the north wall, indicating that the building now had five deeper bays, the easternmost providing an extended presbytery, the extent of which was marked by a step. To the west of this step, at the junction between the original church and the new work were doors in both the north and south walls, that on the north going into a new chapter house while that on the south led into a chapel in range of chapels and vestry which were built against the south side of the church. This addition, which could also be accessed from the lesser cloister was conveniently butted against the old church but bonded with the new east end, showing that it was contemporary with the extension of the church. The chapel closest to the church was vaulted, which suggests it had another room above, while the second chapel was fitted with a secondary spiral staircase, again suggesting an upper floor. Similar two-storey 'towers' appear at London and Mount Grace attached to the side of the church, and this may be a development of what happened at Beauvale. The provision of chapel space outside the presbytery of the church in a Carthusian context is not related to the need to say personal masses, but to something that became central to Carthusian life in the later fourteenth century, the saying of masses for the dead. Almost certainly, what caused the alteration of the church at Beauvale was the influence of patrons and not the immediate needs of the community.

The internal planning of the church can be reconstructed from the evidence of its plan uncovered by excavation. The monks' choir stalls must have been immediately to the west of the doors below the presbytery step, but have terminated at the rood screen that crossed the church to the east of the tomb recesses present in both the north and south walls. Their locations mark the altars that flanked the entrance into the choir. To the west of these altars, occupying the western one and a half bays of the building, was the lay brethren' choir. If the wide north door at the west end of the church was the monks' entrance from the cloister, the narrow southern door from the little cloister must have served the lay brethren.

The churches of Witham, Hinton, and Beauvale, all essentially rectangular churches with no formal division into two parts forming churches for separate groups of monks and lay brethren, make a distinctive group that had ceased to be the pattern from the 1370s. Later churches were all divided by a cross-passage which formed the division between the monks' choir and the lay brethren' church in the nave. The earliest instance of this is found in the church of the London charterhouse.

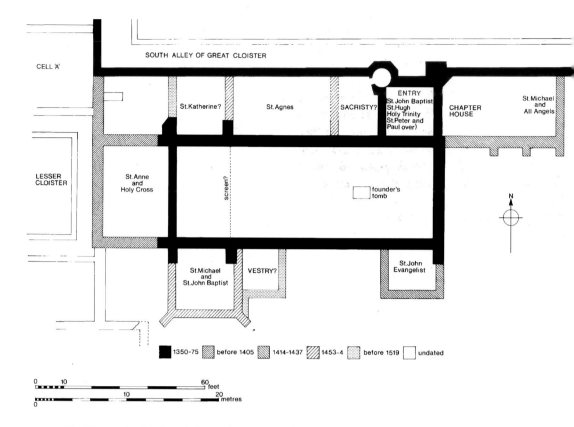

22 *Plan of the church and chapter house at London*

The church at London

Most historians have assumed that the original church of the London charterhouse was the chapel built in the plague cemetery by Bishop Ralph de Stratford in the early 1350s, and that it was simply taken over by the Carthusians when they were given the site in 1371. If they had taken the time to look at the 1430s plan of the London charterhouse however they would have realized that de Stratford's church, the Pardon Chapel, lay just to the north of the charterhouse. The plan of the charterhouse church recovered by excavation, a plain rectangle measuring 27.4 x 9.1m, is remarkably like the other churches raised by the order in England, and it was found to be of one build with a two-storey tower-like structure at its north-east corner that joined with the great cloister of the charterhouse (**22**). The western bay, marked externally by buttresses that were otherwise only used on the corners of the building, was the location of the rood screen, and there was a passage through the church immediately to its west. The west wall of the church was a temporary blocking, much narrower than the other walls of the church, and it was always intended that the nave of the church would be extended to the west to create a lay brethren's church, something achieved before 1405. It is this church which is shown on the waterworks plan of the 1430s in elevation with gable crosses, a steeply pitched lead roof, and a centrally placed octagonal bell-cote and steeple above the monks' choir **(colour plate 20)**. This last feature stood upon the roof and must have been of timber, for it has left no trace on the ground.

Unlike all the earlier churches, the London church was expanded laterally throughout the life of the monastery. The first extension was a small chapel on the south side of the presbytery built between 1414-37, and dedicated to St John the Evangelist. This was followed by a larger chapel to St Agnes, built in the garden or court that separated the church from the great cloister, with a possible sacristy to its east, and a second chapel on the south side of the lay brethren' church dedicated to St Michael and St Jerome, built by Sir John Popham before 1453/4. A fourth chapel was added to the west of St Agnes' chapel before 1519, together with a vestry on the south side of the church. The reason for building in every case was to provide space for lay burials, which brought bequests with them and provided support for the monks who were requested (and paid) to say obituary masses. Although far removed from Prior Guigues de St-Romain's twelfth-century constitutions for the order, which forbade lay burial primarily because of the obligations that came with it, this was a mark of the popularity of the Carthusians and the perceived power of their prayers.

The twelfth-century constitutions set down very clearly how a Carthusian church should be decorated and furnished. Specifically, Prior Guigues wrote 'ornaments of gold and silver, except the chalice and reed by which we take the Lord's Blood, we do not have in the church; hangings and carpets we have given up'. Altars were to have simple wooden crosses, and the painted decoration so common with the Benedictines and Cluniacs was rejected. In this, the Carthusians followed the simplicity of the early Cistercians; but what the rule required and what actually happened was very different, and there must have been a progressive slide from rigid compliance to what is actually recorded in the early sixteenth century. We are remarkably fortunate to have a contemporary description of the London church made by Drs Thomas Legh, and Francis Cave in 1539:

> The Quere
> The hyghe alter of the storye of the passyon of bowne [? ivory], wrought wyth smalle Imagys Curyouslie, at ether end of the sayd alter an Image the on of saint John Baptyste and the other of saint Peter and above the sayd alter iij tabernacles, the nether fronte of the alter of alabaster wyth the Trinitie and other Imagys, at the South Syde of the same at thende of the alter a Cupparde painted wyth the pycture of Cryste. On the northe syde of the alter an ambry wyth a letter. In the same quere a lampe and a bason to bere waxe both of latten, the Stalles of the sayd quere on ether syde wyth a lectern, undefacyd.

Saint Johns Chappell
In the Southe syde of the Churche a chappell of saint John thavaungelyste wyth an alter and a table of the Resurrecyon of alabaster with ij Imagys of saint John Evaungellyst and the other of saint Augustyne at eyther ende of the said alter.

Item the sayd chappel is scealyd wyth oke waynscotte and other borde Rounde abougte thre quarters hygh.

The bodye of the Churche
The Rodelofte wyth an Image of Cryste Crusyfyed a mownteyne with ij alters on eyther syde of the quere dore. On the southe syde an alter with a table of the assumption of Our Lady gylte there remaynynge.

The chapell of saint Jerome
An alter table wythe a Crucyfyx of Marye and John. ij Imagys at ether ende of the sayd alter, the one of Irone (Jerome) the other of saint Barnard, the sayd Chappell being partelye scelyd wyth wayn skotte.

Item ij seates and a lyttell Coffer.

[no heading]

Item. An alter of St Mychell wythe a ffayre table of the Crucyfyx marye and John and at eyther ende of thalter an Image the on of Seint Mychell thother of saint John.

Mr Redys Chappell
An alter wythe a table of the Trinite the iij Doctors of the Churche the same chappell beinge selyd wyth waynskot and ij Covers all remaynynge undefaced.

Item nyghe unto the sayd Chappell a pewe wyth ij seates of waynscott.

The North syde of the Quere
An alter wythe a table of saynt anne gylte wyth certeyn other Imagys gylt and payntyd. Item a table wyth an auter of saint anne and owr ladye with certeyn other Imagys above the sayd alter at ether ende an Image wyth a tabernacle and betwyxte every on of the sayd alters above wrytten there ys a partysyon of waynskotte.

The weste end of the Church
On the north syde an alter in the myddes of mary and John, fayer paynted. Item on the southe syde an alter wyth a table of the passyon of Cryste fayr painted.

Item in the myddes of the sayd ende a particion of tymber wyth pykes of Iron above.

Also in the nave were 'vij Seatys and settells' for the lay brethren whose church this was. Additionally, Dr Richard Leyton removed 12 chalices, a cencer, a pyx, an incence boat, 22 cruets, reliquaries of St Sithe and St Barbara, two paxes, and eight spoons, in all some 4047 ounces of silver from the church. To this can be added rich altar cloths and vestments, Turkish carpets, and cushions. Clearly the Carthusians of London furnished their churches and dressed their altars in much the same way as anyone else at this time. The likelihood is that a considerable proportion of these items comprised gifts to the house that it would be difficult to refuse.

The church at Coventry

The London charterhouse was a rich institution, funded by courtiers, bishops, and the merchant class. Coventry was a royal foundation by adoption and was similarly supported by Bishop Bokingham of Lincoln, and the town had its rich merchants who flocked to support it. The church, however, developed very differently here; that begun in 1385 when Richard II laid the foundation stone was presumably not the first church but replaced a temporary building (**23**). It was 26.5m long and 8m wide, with a narrow stone east wall that the excavator concluded was a temporary structure. No west wall was traced, and this was presumed to be a temporary closure awaiting the later construction of the nave. Essentially, all that was built in the first phase was the monks' choir and a short presbytery to house the altar. The progress was controlled by the raising of funds for the church: Richard Luff and John Botener of Coventry and John Holmeton of Sleaford all made generous

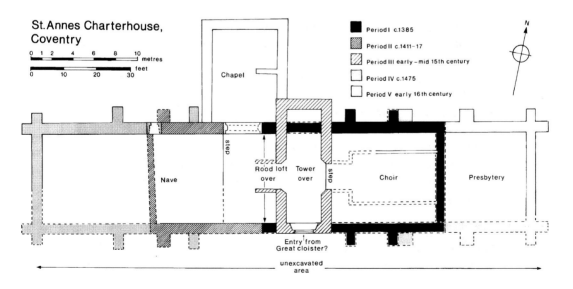

23 *Plan of the church at Coventry*

grants towards the building of the choir, while Dame Margaret Tilney gave £10 towards the window 'at the end of the choir'. The church was extended westward between 1411-17, though this extension was only a partial building of what was intended. Its west wall comprised a narrow foundation that again signified a temporary closure.

This simple rectangular church had a passage through in the third bay from the east, originally marked by the pulpitum screen to the east and the rood screen to the west, and with a loft above. It was the entrance to the monks' church from the great cloister and was derived from the planning of the friars' churches, where a similar arrangement appeared by the second half of the thirteenth century. It was not a purely English arrangement, for this form of double screen with a loft above and altars below facing into the nave can be found in the charterhouses of Cologne, Nuremberg, Gdansk, Basle, Ittingen, and Jülich. In the early to mid-thirteenth century the Coventry community rebuilt their passage in stone, with a broad door in its south wall leading from the great cloister and a projection on the north side of the church that must have contained a stair. Why it was rebuilt in masonry remains unclear; only the foundations remain and there are no convenient contemporary illustrations. It is, however, virtually contemporary with an almost identical arrangement at Mount Grace, and the excavators concluded that it was to carry a centrally placed stone tower, an improvement on the wood and lead steeple of the London church. The west wall was still essentially the rood screen, and narrow cills projecting westwards defined chapels to either side of the central door, and helped to support the rood loft that overlooked the nave.

The rebuilding of the passage did not complete the church, and it was not until the 1470s that the nave was completed and the presbytery lengthened by one and a half bays to the east. Only at this point could the monks' choir stalls be fitted in their final form, extending from the east wall of the passage to the line of the original east wall. The buttresses on the north side of the church, the only ones seen in excavation, were rearranged to provide regular bay spacings, and this means that the windows in the side walls were either moved or replaced in the late fifteenth century. The extension of the church to east and west was a major undertaking. The final development in the early sixteenth century was a double chapel built against the north side of the nave. Because the church at Coventry has been substantially excavated to modern standards, it is possible to see how and why the church was extended. It was not that space was required for liturgy, the normal reason in other orders for the extension or remodeling of the churches, but for burial. The architectural fragments recovered from the church indicate that it was a fine building, with elaborate traceried windows and screens. Its floor was covered with highly decorated floor tiles (**24**), some of them heraldic and recording patrons real or appropriated, others geometric or floral, and its windows were filled with pictorial glass. The walls, to judge from the masonry recovered, were simply painted with white limewash.

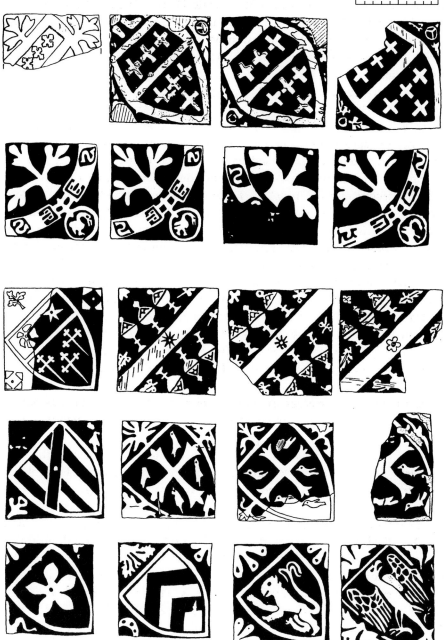

24 *Floor tiles from the church at Coventry*

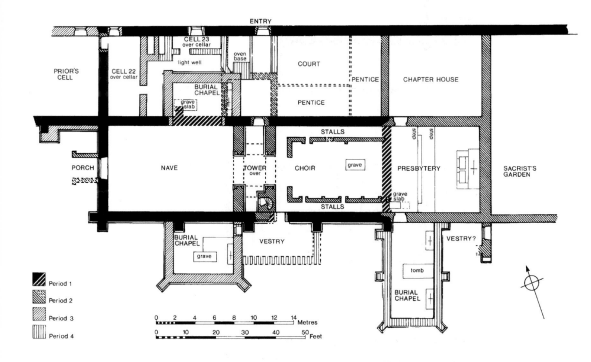

25 *Plan of the church and chapter house at Mount Grace*

The church at Mount Grace

In contrast Mount Grace, the latest surviving Carthusian church in England, is well preserved and the greater part of it stands almost to full height. It was excavated in the late 1890s and cleared of fallen debris in the 1960s, but it has never been examined below the level of its latest floors (**25**; **colour plate 5**). What is known about it comes from a detailed study of its surviving fabric in the late 1980s, and by a study of the loose architectural fragments that came from it. There are four phases of construction (**26**); the first a simple rectangular church of four bays, measuring 28m x 7.3m internally with a narrow screened passage at the west end of its second bay from the east; the second with an extended presbytery and the passage replaced with screen walls that carry a small but elaborate bell-tower, as well as a two-storey block of chapels built on the north side and a porch over the west door; a third phase saw chapels added to both sides of the nave, first to the south and then to the north; and the fourth phase involved the creation of a large chapel on the south side of the monks' choir.

The original structure was very similar to the original London church, and an early fifteenth century drawing of St Bruno and the first community of the Grande Chartreuse made at Mount Grace almost certainly shows this church as it was built (**colour plate 1**). Only three bays are depicted, each with a traceried window, and set on the roof is a small bell-cote with a lead-covered spirelet. Divided into four bays by buttresses, this church had four elaborate traceried windows of a very unusual

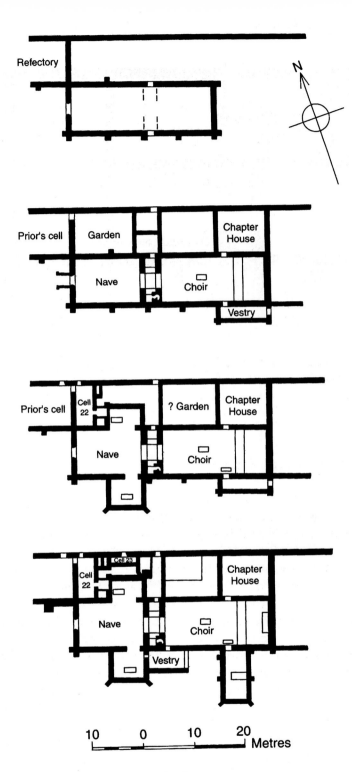

26 *Phased plan of the Mount Grace church*

27 *The monks entrance to the Mount Grace church*

design in its south wall, and a fifth in the eastern bay of its north wall. If there was a west window it was replaced by a larger one in the course of the fifteenth century. Small doors, not exactly aligned, marked the passage through the church at the west end of the monks' choir, and there was a stoup for Holy Water next to the north door by which the monks entered their church (**27**). The church was built throughout of squared stone, unlike the rubble of Beauvale, and the blocks were left roughly dressed to assist the keying of plaster. Tracery recovered from the south side of the church enables the missing windows to be reconstructed (**28**), and this has allowed comparison with other contemporary churches in the region. The closest parallels are to be found not in a monastic context but in parish churches; two churches are particularly close in detail, those of Burneston **(colour plate 6)** and Catterick. Both are the work of a known mason, Richard de Cracall, who also seems to have been associated with

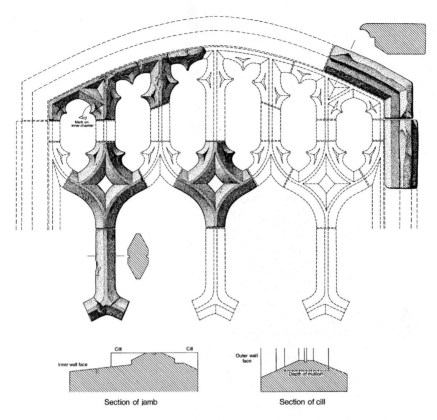

Section of jamb Section of cill

28 *Reconstructed window of c.1400*

this church in its early phases. It is perhaps surprising that a relatively unknown local mason, as opposed to someone closely related to the Office of Works or Westminster, should build the church of a monastery founded by a central member of the royal court; but it may be that Thomas de Holand provided the money and the community was responsible for contracting the work. Richard de Cracall was known in monastic circles. He built the chancel at Burneston for St Mary's Abbey at York.

The second phase of building can be directly associated with the patronage of Thomas Beaufort, who obtained a license to be buried in this church in 1417 and who was indeed interred there ten years later. He increased the size of the community from 12 to 18, and it is uncertain whether the extension of the building was necessitated by the growth of the community or the need to provide the patron with a fitting burial place. First, the timber screens of the passage were removed, to be replaced by stone screen walls that rose the full height of the church to carry an exquisite bell-tower (**29**). The northern door of the old passage had to be moved slightly to the west, and the southern door was blocked up permanently by the spiral stair that gave access to the tower. The reason for the tower, apart from raising the status of the church, was to house at least two bells rather than the single bell needed to call the community to church. Both survived the suppression, one going to

29 *The bell tower at Mount Grace*

Northallerton where it was broken and recast in 1802; the other was still in use in Osmotherley church in 1895 when it too was recast.

As the tower at Mount Grace is the only Carthusian tower to survive in England, its origins are important. There is, in fact, an almost contemporary tower in the Franciscan friary in Richmond **(colour plate. 7)**, so close in detail to the bell-tower here to be either the model for it or a copy of it. Others survive in the grey friars churches of Kings Lynn and Coventry, and just as the passage through the later Carthusian churches was modeled on the 'walking space' at the west end of the friars' choir, so the screen walls and central tower seem to have been adopted from the friars' churches.

Contemporary with the building of the tower was the eastward extension of the presbytery. New windows were provided high up in the north wall of the choir, and grooves cut into the wall face indicate the tall backs of new canopied stalls. As at Beauvale, opposed doors were placed at the junction of the old and new work, that on the north going into the chapter house, that on the south into a vestry. Late

30 *Evidence for the choir roof*

nineteenth-century photographs (**30**) show surviving limewash on the east wall of the tower that marks the curving ceiling of the choir, which must have been boarded out in imitation of a barrel vault. The east window of the new extension has been recovered, showing that this too was the work of Richard de Cracall (**31**). At the same time, a two-storey block was built between the church and the great cloister. Its ground floor provided the entry into the church and possible chapel space; there were certainly chapels on the first floor because a piscina survives in the north wall of the church. This structure occupies the same space as the 'low tower' at London, but here it was not a tower. The block had a steeply pitched roof, the mark of which can still be seen on the side of the church.

In the 1470s, a square chapel was built on the south side of the nave, connected to the church by the simple expedient of taking out the window in that bay and cutting the wall down to floor level. Lit by large windows in its south and west walls, it contains a substantial tomb. It is not known who is buried here, and there are probably many more graves below the stone floor. It was followed by a slightly smaller chapel on the north side of the church, the construction of which entailed the demolition of the two-storey block over the monks' entry. Here, because there was no window, a tall segmental-arched opening was cut in the nave wall. There is a single gravestone visible in the floor. Both chapels had altars against their window-less east walls where the sockets remain for tall reredoses. Between the two chapels on the west wall of the tower are the fixings for a rood loft with a pair of altars to either side of the central arch. If the nave was the church of the lay brethren, the side

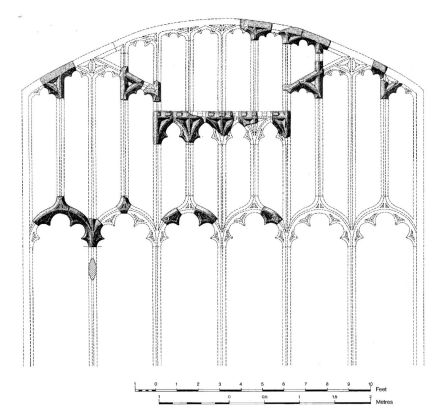

Feet

Metres

31 *Reconstructed east window*

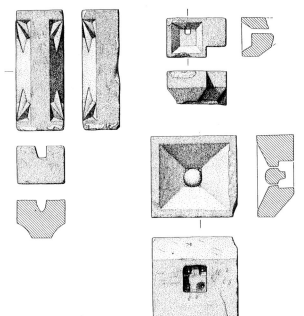

32 *Piscinas from the eastern chapel*

At þe begynyng of þe chartur hous god dyd schewe
To þe bysshop of grachonapolitane þaynt Hewe
Seuen sternes goyng i dildines to þat place
Wher now þe ordir of þe chartur hous abydyng has
And Aŧon per stres at þat place had bene
At þe bisshops Aete yai Aelto al bedene
And aftyr yis visione þe sothe for to saye
þe Doctor Bruno t six felos ŧ onton delay
Come to yis holy bisshop counsel take
To lyf solytary i dildines ŧ þis warld to forsake
And at his Aete mekly done yai Aolle
Askyng hym of Tformacon t his counsell to telle
Than conseyd he wole þe vision of þe seuen sternes þ he saue
þus þe doctor of diuinite Bruno ŧ his six felos cryng outas
ŧ God þis seuen sternes synyfyes yis seuen þsons alle
Askyng hym of his Aet ayog almyȝty god sno calle

1 *The foundation of La Grande Chartreuse from a miscellany written at Mount Grace Priory.*
British Library Ms 37049 f22

2 *The chapter house at Hinton seen across the site of the church*

3 *The church at Beauvale*

4 *The great terrace on which Mount Grace charterhouse was built from 1398*

5 *The church at Mount Grace.* English Heritage

6 *Richard de Cracall's east window at Burneston, closely parallel to the windows of his church at Mount Grace*

7 *The tower of the Franciscan friary at Richmond, Yorkshire, which provides the model for the Mount Grace tower (or vice versa)*

8 *Cell 10 at Mount Grace, where excavation revealed the slots that contained the joists of a wooden floor.* Richard Hall

9 *The latrine gallery in Cell 8 at Mount Grace in the course of reconstruction*

10 *The garden of Cell 9 at Mount Grace under excavation.* Laurence Keen

11 *The late fifteenth-century garden of Cell 8 at Mount Grace*

12 *The pardon panel from Cell 10 at Mount Grace.* Richard Hall

13 *The cloister laver at Mount Grace*

14 *The library (left) and prison (right) in the west range of the great cloister at Mount Grace*

15 *The early prior's cell at Mount Grace*

16 *The kitchen at Mount Grace in the course of excavation. The dark areas on the floor are deposits of food waste*

17 *The London charterhouse plan showing the springs that supplied water to the house and the first conduit house.* English Heritage

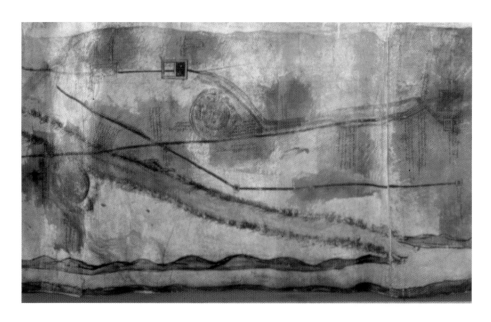

18 *The London charterhouse plan showing the home pipe and second conduit house.* English Heritage

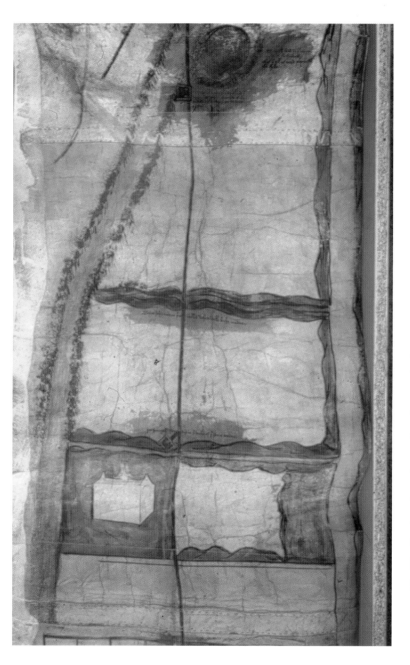

19 *The London charterhouse plan showing the home pipe and the cemetery chapel to the north of the charterhouse.* English Heritage

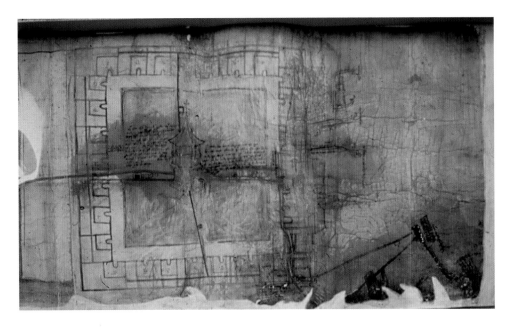

20 *The London charterhouse plan showing the water tower, the distribution of water within the house, and the flesh kitchen.* English Heritage

21 *The water tower at Mount Grace in the course of excavation. The wooden piles on which the tower stood can clearly be seen*

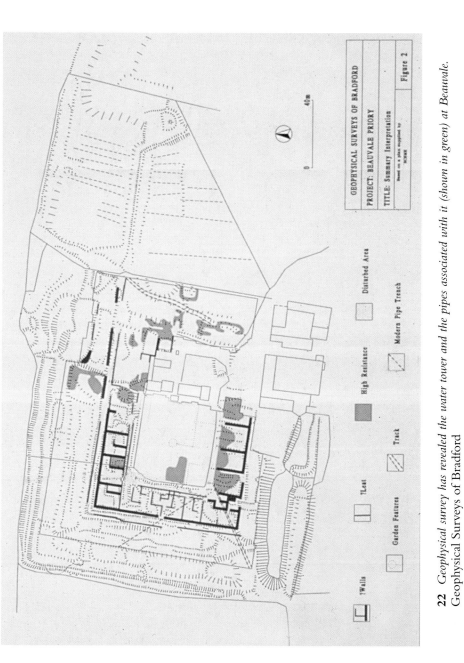

22 *Geophysical survey has revealed the water tower and the pipes associated with it (shown in green) at Beauvale.*
Geophysical Surveys of Bradford

23 *The post suppression house built from the prior's cell and refectory at Coventry*

33 *Reconstruction of the Mount Grace church*

chapels were for the saying of masses for the dead, just like the chapels of St Michael and St Katherine which occupy the same positions in London.

In the early sixteenth century, a third chapel was added to the south side of the presbytery, requiring the removal of the vestry of the 1420s. This new chapel contained two altars separated by a chest tomb, the base of which survives. A further burial was placed in the floor of the presbytery in front of the door into this chapel. Again, the purpose of this chapel was the saying of mortuary masses, for when it was excavated in the 1890s it produced two piscinas for the washing of mass vessels (**32**). By the suppression, the church at Mount Grace had changed out of all recognition from the simple rectangular church of 1400, in almost exactly the same ways as the London church (**33**). They are so similar that they must have been developed to a common plan.

Burials in English charterhouses

Choir monks and lay brethren were normally buried in the cloister garth, uncoffined and wrapped in their habits, their cemetery only taking up a part of the area. With the exception of five graves that were located but not excavated at London, no

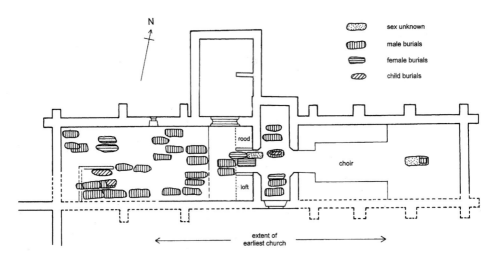

34 *Burials in the church at Coventry*

Carthusian cemetery has been examined in Britain, or indeed anywhere else. Priors were not always buried with their community, but occasionally in the cloister alley closest to the church, where burials have been found at London and Mount Grace. In the latter location, the two burials that have been examined (one outside the door to the prior's early cell and one below the cloister laver) were not marked by grave slabs but simply sealed by the alley floor. They were also uncoffined, and neither contained the mortuary chalice and patten of lead normally found with a priest's burial. At London, excavation revealed three large, plain grave markers in the tiled floor of the south cloister alley outside St Katherine's chapel, as well as two smaller slabs which may cover heart or viscera burials. The fact that the grave slabs were not inscribed or decorated suggests that they were not patronal burials, but they were left undisturbed when the area was excavated and their identity has to remain unkown.

Founders were normally buried in the church in the monks' choir between their stalls or before the high altar, where they shared the prayers of the community. Excavation at London revealed a brick-lined grave in this latter location still containing the lead-wrapped body of Sir Walter Maney, while at Mount Grace the base of Thomas Beaufort's altar-tomb can yet be seen at the centre of the choir, off-set to the north to avoid the earlier burial of Thomas de Holand (**25**). A similarly placed grave at Beauvale probably marks the burial of Sir Nicholas de Cantilupe (**21**).

At Coventry the burial pattern has been recovered for the whole church (**34**). A very strange grave was dug immediately in front of the altar when the church was extended to the east in the late fifteenth century. The grave pit was clearly dug for a wooden coffin of full size but that coffin, though placed in the grave, did not contain a body. Instead, at the its foot was a wooden casket that contained the fragmentary remains of a middle-aged man who had previously been buried elsewhere. This is possibly the founder William, Lord Zouch, who having died a century earlier and before the church was actually begun, was finally buried before the high altar of his charterhouse.

The appeal of the Carthusians to the laity placed incredible pressure on the order to accept lay burials in their churches. Bodies came for interment accompanied by grants of land or fees for masses and obits, but they required space that was at a premium in small Carthusian churches. They also disturbed the exclusivity of the community, but were a direct result of the monks' spirituality. The answer was compromise, with churches being extended to provide burial space, as at Beauvale, London and Mount Grace with additional altars at which commemorative masses could be said. On the whole, lay burial (except for patrons) avoided the monks' choir, indicating that the monks were happy to accept lay burials but not in their own part of the church.

While it is clear that burials were intended in the Beauvale church, and two grave recesses were provided in the nave from its time of building or shortly after, it was the added chapels on the south side of the presbytery that contained the only interments traced by the excavators. The tile floor of the northern chapel had been disturbed by repeated burials marked not by ledger slabs, but with reset tiles which had subsided into the grave fill.

The best evidence for lay burials comes from Coventry, where the greater part of the church has been fully excavated (**34**). Although this included only a third of the choir and a half of the presbytery, the pattern of burial is probably complete. A total of 39 graves was excavated, one (described above) in the presbytery, six below the tower in front of the original pulpitum screen, five at the entrance to the monks' choir in front of or below the rood screen and loft, and 28 in the body of the nave, 15 of which lay in the fifteenth-century extension added to the west. The early sixteenth-century chapel on the north side of the nave was almost certainly built to take further burials, but none had taken place there before the suppression. Several graves had been reused, and were probably family plots, and some had been reopened to bury children. In all, the remains of 29 men, five women, and seven children were identified, with a further six being too fragmentary to identify. Slightly less than half of the adult burials were coffined, and only one, a female buried centrally below the rood screen, lay in a stone-lined grave. Some graves had been marked in the tile floor of the church by the resetting of disturbed floor tiles, and at least one group of three burials – that of John Fitzherbert and his parents – is known to have been marked by a ledger stone. This was probably one of the reused graves rather than a stone covering three individual burials. Additionally, excavation has recovered part of a tomb chest, suggesting that some burials were marked above floor level.

Who was buried in the church at Coventry? Only John Langley, lord of Shortley, Thomas Bickley and Margaret Warton of Coventry, and Nicholas Fitzherbert are known by name. The westernmost burial on the south side of the nave was a priest, for he was buried with a chalice of Venetian glass; and one, the most westerly on the north side of the nave, was an executed felon, for his body had been quartered. Most likely, the others were local landowners and the leading members of city guilds, certainly not the urban poor, or the house's principal patrons who were buried elsewhere.

At London, limited excavation revealed that burials outside the choir and presbytery were similar to the pattern seen at Coventry. Immediately west of the monks' choir, within the passage through the church, the graves were tightly packed as though this was a favoured location. Unfortunately, the remainder of the nave was not examined. Built tombs were found in many of the chapels, almost certainly provided at the time of building for their sponsors, and in St Michael's chapel in addition to Sir John Popham's tomb an earth-dug grave immediately to the south of it was recorded in the limited area excavated.

At Mount Grace, where burial had forced the community to extend their church substantially, the evidence is clear that interment was restricted to those who were able to make substantial contributions to the house. In 1432, William de Authorp, rector of Kirk Deighton and a kinsman of John de Ingleby the joint founder, desired to be buried in the church at Mount Grace, and he left to the prior and convent a silver cup, 12 silver spoons, and a book called *Pupilla occuli*. In 1436, Thomas Lokwood of East Harlsey Grange, a tenant of Rievaulx Abbey, willed 20s and requested that his body be buried in the church at Mount Grace, while in July 1438, Eleanor de Roos was buried there and left to the convent a silver vessel with a cover, and a noble apiece to the other seven English charterhouses. Joan Ingleby, widow of Sir William Ingleby, died in October 1478, and though she made no pecuniary bequest to the convent, she willed her body for burial there, suggesting that she or her husband had supported the community while alive. In 1483 Christopher Conyers, chaplain and rector of Rudby also requested interment there and left 20s to Mount Grace among with many other bequests to religious houses, while Robert Kirton of Crathorne simply willed 'my body to be beryd at Mountegrace'. Thomas Darell of Sessay willed his body to Mount Grace in April 1500, and for that privilege gave 'to the prior and convent my lands and tenements at East Harlsey'. He also willed that two priests should celebrate a mass for his soul for seven years, for which he paid 8 marks. In September 1532, two Strangwayes burials were willed to Mount Grace. On 2 September, Sir Thomas Stangwayes of Harlsey Castle desired

> to be beriede at Mountgrace where as the Prior of the same house thynkes best. Also I gif to my corseprisaunce my best horse. Also I give to the Mountgrace, if it please God that I be beriede there, on other horse. Also I gif to the saide house of Mountgrace, and the brether of the same, for to pray for my saull, 60s. Also I will that the Prior of the Mountgrace have, to pray for my saull and Cristen saulles that God wold have praid for 20s.

Six days later, James Strangwayes of Westlathes in Whorlton parish willed 'to bee tumulate in the monasterie of the Mountgrace, and therfore I yeve theme 20s in money'. The Strangwayes family were important local patrons.

35 *The chapter house at Hinton*

Chapter houses

The chapter house where faults were confessed, punishment given, and the business of the monastery transacted was in the monasteries of other orders second only in importance to the church, and was typically placed in the east range of the cloister. In most orders, it was also the burial place of the abbots or priors whose graves only moved to the church when the chapter house had filled up. In charterhouses, chapter meetings were held weekly, after Prime on Sundays or major festivals, and was restricted to the choir monks. Because the priests in the community were required to say Mass after chapter meetings, the chapter house needed to be close to the church, and the favoured location for it was between the church and the great cloister. Only four chapter houses are known in England; the early thirteenth-century example at Hinton that survives almost intact, and fragmentary buildings of the fourteenth and early fifteenth centuries at London, Beauvale and Mount Grace.

The chapter house at Hinton (**20** & **35**, **colour plate 2**) lay on the east side of the little cloister immediately north of the great cloister's north alley, and could be entered from either the little cloister – the principal entrance – or the church. Originally merely two bays long and lit only by a triplet of lancet windows in its east gable, it was extended by a bay in the middle of the thirteenth century, the east window being reset, and side windows provided in the new eastern bay. In its final form, it was 11.5m long and 5m wide internally. Its west wall does not have the typical central door flanked by open two-light windows favoured by other orders in the twelfth and thirteenth centuries, but a plain moulded door little different from any other in the monastery. Inside, however, the importance of the building is emphasized by a ribbed vault similar to that of the church supported on filleted wall-shafts rising from a half-round stringcourse 1.5m above the floor (**36**). The walls above the stringcourse and the vault retain their original plaster and plain white liming, while below it the side walls are of good-quality ashlar against which monks' benches were placed. Pin holes in the wall show that the top rail of the benches was placed just below the stringcouse. Where the prior's seat would be expected in the centre of the east wall, however, is the base of an altar, with associated piscina and wall-cupboard to south and north, a common provision in Carthusian charterhouses that is rare in other orders. Whether the chapter house was lengthened in order to introduce the altar or simply to provide additional space for the community is uncertain. A second altar outside the church had been agreed at the General Chapter of the order in 1250, but it is quite possible that the legislation was simply autho-rizing something which had already been in use.

Above the chapter house and accessed by a spiral stair against the church wall was another vaulted room of two bays, originally lit by single lancet windows in its east and west walls. Here there is no stringcourse in the walls, and the vault is carried on short wall-shafts that rise from moulded corbels. The rubble walls were originally plastered, and slight traces remain of a more elaborate decorative scheme than that evidenced below in the chapter house. The walls had been whitelimed, but a masonry pattern had been superimposed to give the impression of ashlar work. This was a common scheme in monastic buildings of other orders, particularly those of the Cistercians and Augustinians; but by the thirteenth century the lining was normally done in red paint. Here, a distinctly old-fashioned decorative scheme with white lines had been used. This room, fireproofed by a vaulted ceiling below and above, was the charterhouse library. It sadly retains no evidence for the presses that lined its walls.

Separating the chapter house block from the church was a small sacristy which clearly contained a small altar, because there is a piscina in its south wall.

The London chapter house survives within the sixteenth-century house built on the south side of the great cloister by Lord North, and was a fifteenth-century building of three slightly unequal bays, 6.4m long and 3.2m wide internally, butted against the east side of the low tower on the north-east corner of the church from which it was entered (**22**). It was only a single storey building, for its roof is shown on the 1430s waterworks drawing immediately above the south wall of the great cloister, and it can only have been lit from the south and east sides. From documentary sources we know it had an altar against its east wall dedicated to St Michael and All Saints.

The chapter houses of Beauvale (**21**) and Mount Grace (**25**) are sufficiently similar to discuss together. Both are reduced to low walling, and all that is known about them is their general plan. As both butted against the presbytery of the church, they must have been single storey structures if they were not to interfere with the windows that lit the north side of the presbytery. Both could be entered from the church by a door below the presbytery step, and also had a separate access; at Mount Grace from

36 *Inside the Hinton chapter house*

the court on the north side of the church, and at Beauvale from a long corridor that ran along the north wall of the church from the north-east corner of the great cloister. Both appear to have been closely associated with the sacrist's cell, and at Mount Grace, the sacrist could enter the chapter house directly from the garden gallery of his cell by a door in the east wall. Though the door no longer exists, the steps down to the lower level of the chapter house floor remain in place. It can only have been lit by windows high in its gable walls, for almost half of the east wall was covered by the sacrist's gallery and there was a gallery with a double pitch roof against its west wall. Neither chapter house retains obvious features, indeed that at Beauvale was reburied after excavation and the only indication of its existence is the excavators' plan. It is certain that the Mount Grace chapter house had a wooden roof and no vault, and this seems to be the case at Beauvale. Clearly, the chapter house had fallen in importance since the thirteenth century in England.

4 The Carthusian cell and cloister

Normally, medieval monks lived communally, their beds placed down either side of a great dormitory that occupied the east range of the cloister with one stair leading down into the church for the night offices, and another to the cloister alley. The cloister itself was their living room, and it was here that they studied and copied manuscripts, washed, and even did their laundry. It was a silent place, except for the west alley where novices were taught, and a small room was provided below the dormitory and next to the chapter house where they could talk for limited periods. Also below the dormitory was the day room where they could work within the confines of the cloister. Here, too, was the warming house where the chill of the cloister alleys could be relieved between 1 November and Good Friday.

None of these features appears in a Carthusian monastery. Instead, Carthusian monks lived the life of hermits in separate houses or cells, following the examples of St Anthony and the *lauras* of Egypt and the eastern Mediterranean, and their cloister was simply a gallery connecting a series of miniature monasteries with the church and communal buildings.

Origins

At the initial settlement of the Grande Chartreuse, before the community had begun to develop a rule to govern its life, each cell might be occupied by two monks, a practice which continued up to 1131, for Bishop Hugh de Chateau-Neuf of Grenoble regularly visited and shared a cell until his death in that year. It may have been the reconstruction of the first monastery in the following year that set the pattern for the future. Certainly by the time that Prior Guigues de Saint-Romain framed his *Constitutions* for the growing order in 1128, the idea of individual cells was becoming fixed. The planning of these early cells is quite unknown, for none have survived or been excavated, but their contents are included in Prior Guigues' *Constitutions*. Each monk was to have straw, a felt cloth, a cushion, a covering of coarsest sheepskin and a coverlet of rustic cloth for his bed; he should have two hair shirts, two tunics, two pilches, two cowls, three pairs of breeches, four pairs of socks, a hood, shoes for night and day use, two loin-cloths, and a girdle for his wardrobe; and for his personal needs two needles, thread, scissors, and a razor and strop. Additionally, he was to have the necessary pots, pans, and platters for cooking, wood for his fire, and an axe to cut it with. For writing, he should have a desk, pens, chalk, two pumices, two ink-horns, a pen-knife, two knives for scraping parchment, a parchment pricker and lead dry points, a ruler, and a pencil. He also had the tools of his chosen trade. The cell was to provide for all of the monk's needs and he should have no reason to leave it.

Early Carthusian cells in England

Apart from the briefest references to the temporary wooden cells surrounded by a ditch and fence that greeted Hugh of Avalon when he arrived at Witham in 1180, and to the cells he built around a new great cloister, apparently also of timber, we know nothing of the first Carthusian cells to be built in England. It is not until the building of Hinton in the late 1220s and early 1230s that we actually find evidence for the form of these buildings. Even then, they are known only from the partial excavation of buildings reduced in many cases to foundation level or below; yet a great number of assumptions have been made about these buildings.

Interpretation of the Hinton cells (**11** & **37a**) is complicated by the way they were excavated, with trenches dug along walls and no attempt to uncover floors. No complete cell plan was recovered, and there was an assumption that walls not recovered in some cells because robber trenches were not identified followed the general layout in other cells where they were located. Timber partitions were not sought, or even, it would appear, anticipated. The excavator claimed that

> the cells are uniformly 31ft 6in wide and rather less in depth. They consist of one large room, 20ft square, the rest of the cell usually forming a peculiar "dog-leg", which measured 8ft at the side and 6ft at the end. It seems probable that this was a pentice, but how it was divided up remains a mystery, as this part of the cell has usually been badly knocked about . . . the large room invariably has the hearth, where it still exists, in the same relative position on the side internal wall.

Although it is never stated, there was an assumption, probably justified, that these stone houses were two-storeyed because later cells were. Each cell was identified by a letter carved into the jamb of its cloister door, and though the modern tradition of identifying cells by a number is now the norm, this was not the case in the Middle Ages.

An examination of the ground plan of Cell 11, the most complete cell plan recovered at Hinton, indicates that a very different interpretation is possible. Critical to the understanding of the plan-form of the building is the location of the chimney stack. In the later medieval Carthusian cell this would be expected to occupy a central position in one of the gable walls of the cell: but at Hinton it does not. It does however lie in every case on the centre line of the building so that the chimney would pass through the ridge-line of the cell, on the line of an internal wall. The cell measured 9.1 x 7.7m internally, of which the living room or hall occupied an area 6.6 x 5.9m. If the fireplace was centrally located in the end wall of the hall, then there

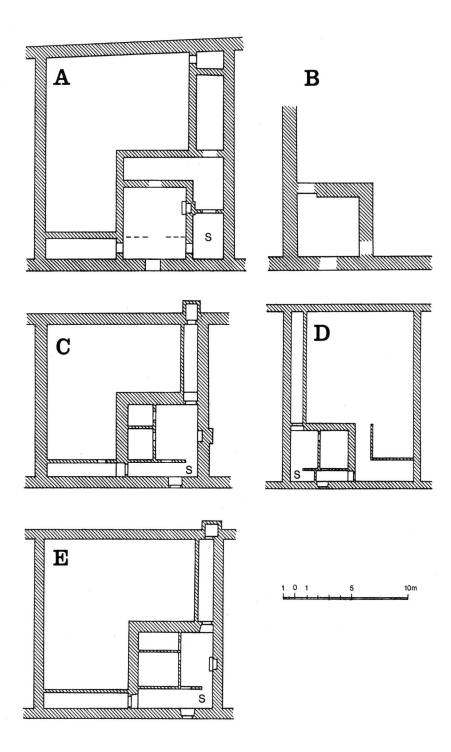

37 *Comparative plans of Carthusian cells*

would have been a lobby some 1.8m wide between the hall and the door from the cloister, and the hall would have been 4.8m wide. There was a door at each end of this lobby in Cell 11, that at the south end leading to an external gallery, but that on the north into the narrow room between the gable wall of the cell and the wall containing the hall fireplace. This space was 2.25m wide. In Cells 3, 4, and 12, a cross wall aligned with the chimney stack defined a room approximately 3m long; in Cells 4 and 12 this wall had a centrally placed door. Because this space can have had no windows at ground floor level its most likely interpretation is as the location of the stair to the upper floor, perhaps with a cupboard below. It most certainly was not a gallery as Fletcher claimed. The other 'corridor' along the garden side of the hall appears never to have been seriously investigated. Where its outer wall was investigated it was found to be the same width as the other external walls of the cell, but its inner wall was thinner, suggesting it was only carried up to the first floor while the wall that contained the chimney flue was carried up to the ridge. The 'corridor' was only 1.4m wide. In Cell 7 there was a centrally placed door from the hall.

On analogy with later cells, two spaces are missing, a room for study and a bedroom which also served as an oratory or private chapel, each of which could have occupied one leg of the 'L'-shaped corridor. The form and use of the upper floor remains unknown, but as each monk had a trade in addition to his profession, it provided a convenient workroom and store. Flanking the cell itself were two galleries, one entered from the passage inside the cloister door and ranged along the cloister wall, the second running along the garden wall from the back of the cell to the boundary wall at the back of the garden. The first was essentially a private 'cloister' that overlooked the garden, the second led to a latrine placed against the boundary wall.

Just as the cells at Hinton are the largest to be found in England, so is their garden area. Unfortunately none of the gardens were examined and we therefore lack the evidence for their cultivation. They had two uses, one practical, the other metaphorical. They provided the monk with the opportunity for manual labour within the confines of his cell, and as a *hortus inclusus* (enclosed garden) they referred directly to the garden of the 'Song of Solomon' with its imagery of the virgin bride and thus the Blessed Virgin Mother of God herself. What Hinton shows is that by the 1220s the standard form of the Carthusian cell had already appeared in England, and though it was to be modified in the fourteenth and fifteenth centuries, its basic components had already been defined.

Later Carthusian cells in England

At present, there is nothing in England with which to compare the Hinton cells and their gardens, for what appeared from the middle years of the fourteenth century is slightly different. This is as true of the continental houses of the order as it is in England, and indicates that the Carthusian cell had developed across the order. Henry Yevely, the King's master mason, was commissioned to build the first cells of the London charterhouse in 1381 and he appears to have introduced the new design to England in a slightly modified form which was to be copied at Beauvale, Coventry and Mount Grace. The one cell excavated at Witham (**37b**) appears to belong to this later series. Why there should be a difference in planning between 'early' and 'late' cells is not known, and it is significant that there was no need to rebuild or modify the cells at Hinton, which continued in their original form into the sixteenth century. The new cell plan came from a non-monastic source, the accommodation of priests in colleges and from lodgings in great houses. Henry Yeveley had designed a different form in 1370-1 for chantry priests at Cobham in Kent, comprising individual cells with a bed chamber and living room; and it was this plan he developed for the London charterhouse.

The London cells were roughly 6.4m² internally and were set in the corner of gardens approximately 14m². None has been completely excavated and their internal planning is unknown. They are shown on the 1430s waterworks drawing, all identified by a letter which was presumably painted on the jamb of the cloister door; in neither of the two door cases which survive is the letter carved into the stonework. Their plan can be reconstructed from what is known of the cells at Beauvale, Coventry, and Mount Grace. The cloister door was placed at the centre of the front wall; next to it was a square hatch which turned through 90 degrees and opened into the door reveal, a standard Carthusian provision which is unrecorded at Hinton because the walls of the cells only survive to a maximum of two or three courses of stone. The purpose of this hatch was for a lay brother or servant to bring food and other requisites without disturbing or even seeing the occupant of the cell. On the garden side of the cell was a second door which led to a gallery along the back of the cloister wall. No back wall was sufficiently examined to locate the third door which led to the latrine, and no masonry internal walls were located, indicating that the ground floor of the cell was divided into rooms by wooden partitions or wainscot. At the suppression it is recorded that 'one of the sayd brederne toke away . . . sertayn boordys of waynscote whyche dyffacyd the Cellys very sore'.

The Mount Grace cells

To understand the form of the later Carthusian cell it is necessary to look to Mount Grace,where there are the remains of 16 standard cells around the great cloister, many standing at least in part to full height and eight of which have been excavated since 1968 (**38**). They range in date from *c.*1400 to the 1470s, are all of two storeys, and all have been altered during their use to suit the needs of individual monks. Apart from two additional later cells which are of non-standard layout, all of the houses share a common plan. They are 6.4m² internally and are set in the corner of the garden, just like the Hinton cells (**37e**). A door normally placed slightly off-centre in the cloister wall with a hatch next to it led into a narrow lobby (**39**), with a door into a gallery along the inside of the cloister wall at one end, and a cupboard at the other, below a wooden stair up to the first floor. Opposite the cloister door was an entrance leading into the living room with a wall fireplace, and another door in the back wall of the cell that led to a latrine at the bottom of the garden through a second gallery or pentice. The stair was entered through the partition wall opposite the door to the latrine. Entered from the living room

38 *Cells around the Mount Grace cloister*

39 *The cloister door and hatch of Cell 4*

40 *The interior of Cell 4*

were two more rooms, a narrow bedroom and oratory and a larger study. The windows survive in the ground floor of Cell 4 at Mount Grace (**40**), though they are replacements of the later fifteenth century: the living room and study were both lit by a large four-light window, while the bedroom had two small single-light windows. These were originally barred and shuttered; the upper lights of the four-light windows were glazed and the lower lights barred and shuttered, though all were later glazed. The upper floor does not appear to have been partitioned, and was normally lit by windows in the gable walls, though in two cases (Cells 10 and 15) there were also windows looking out over the cloister. The upper floor was normally a work-room, though in no case is there any evidence for what it contained or how it was furnished.

Excavation has provided a mass of evidence for the internal appearance of the cells. In many cases, the ground floors were of wood, supported on joists (**colour plate 8**). Brushwood packed beneath the floors was evidently a primitive form of insulation. In several cases, the entry lobby was paved with stone, and this paving continued below the staircase and along the gable wall of the cell to the latrine door, providing a fire-proof area in front of the fireplace. In only one instance – inside the latrine door in Cell 10 – does there appear to have been a tiled floor as opposed to stone paviors. In every case, the internal partitions were of timber supported on carefully cut stone cill walls, and in several cases sockets cut into the cell walls to fix the partitions indicate that these could be moved to change the size of individual rooms. Masonry walls were painted with white limewash, and in some cases plastered. Cell 8 retains evidence for sixteenth-century paneling in its living room.

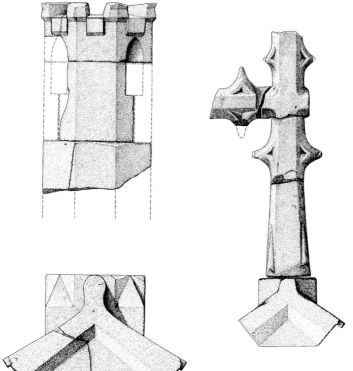

41 *A cell chimney and gable cross*

Although built to a standard plan, no two cells were identical and it would seem that individual monks had them altered to suit their own needs. Indeed, Richard Methley recalled in his book *Refectorium Salutis* (The Restoration of Well-being) praying before an image of the Virgin in his oratory and feeling the wind that entered through a new but unfinished window that 'he had caused to be made to let in more light and air'. In several cases, the wall below a window had been cut back so that the monk could sit in the window reveal, presumably to give him more light for reading and writing.

Elements of architectural detailing survived from almost every cell and enable their reconstruction with remarkable clarity. The four-light windows survive both in position and as loose fragments, and these show that the very latest architectural fashions were being followed by the late fifteenth century. Every cell had a chimney rising from the apex of one of its gables, and many fragments of these have been recovered (**41**). Octagonal in plan, they rose from specially detailed apex stones, and had smoke holes in the form of tiny lancet windows in alternate faces below a moulded and castellated cap. The opposite gable was finished with a cross rising from the apex stone (**41**). In short, the cells were sophisticated houses which were architecturally distinguished

Each cell had two attached galleries that followed the earlier design of Hinton and served the same purpose. By the early years of the fifteenth century they had developed, however, from the stone-built galleries of Hinton to light timber struc-

42 *The garden gallery of Cell 8*

tures set on low plinth walls. In Cell 8 at Mount Grace, sufficient evidence survived to show how the galleries were framed and excavation recovered the graded slates from their roofs, enabling their reconstruction (**42**). The gallery along the cloister wall had a deep wall-plate, its socket cut into the cell wall, and over 600 pieces of glass and the lead cames that had held them were recovered from its windows. The windows probably had arched heads like those of contemporary cloister arcades. Inside, the gallery had a wooden floor and a plastered ceiling. Looking out into the cell garden, it provided the monk with a private cloister where he could read and meditate alone. It is the only one at Mount Grace known to have been glazed, and others did not have the wooden floor; so again, it would seem that individual needs were catered for.

The second gallery that led to the latrine also normally had the door to the garden. Again, that of Cell 8, which was atypical because the cell was placed at the centre of its garden and not in one corner, has been reconstructed by setting its frame into the sockets that survived in the masonry of the cell and garden walls (**colour plate 9**). The same construction, however, was used in every cell – an open wall and a single pitch roof. Because the gallery was not glazed in, a solid floor of gravel was provided, while in other cells, notably 10 and 14, the gallery was floored with stone paviors. It is likely that these were used more widely, but having a resale value they had been removed at the suppression.

The latrines themselves are remarkable structures, and take two forms. The gardens of Cells 1-5 are terraced back into the hillside and it was therefore not possible to build latrines outside the garden walls. They are actually provided within the end of the gallery (**43**), and comprise a deep pit with a wooden seat over it. Alongside the seat is a stone basin that discharges into the pit, providing a place to clean one's hands and wash out the rags that served as toilet paper. The pit itself was set over a carefully constructed sewer, and was fed by spring water from the hillside through a hole in its back wall. At the time that other orders' communal latrines were falling out of use and being replaced by the less hygienic pit latrine, the Carthusians were paying remarkable attention to the disposal of their waste, for almost every latrine at Mount Grace was permanently water-flushed. Cells 6-15 each had a latrine constructed partly inside the garden wall and partly outside it (**44**), with a seat set over a sewer that ran below ground level, and flushed by a stream diverted from the hillside above the house specifically for the purpose. Remarkably every latrine had a lockable door and at least one (Cell 8) had a niche for a candle. The seat was quite wide, and part of it acted as a shelf on which urinals were kept. Urine was not thrown away, but was

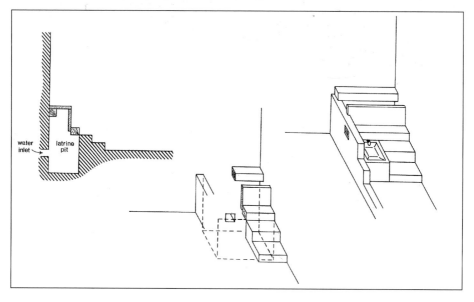

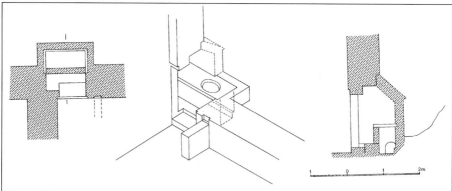

43 & 44 *The latrine of Cells 4 and 7*

45 *Cells 22 and 23*

used in the preparation of parchment and for alchemical research, an interest suggested by the fact that at least one monk at Mount Grace had a still.

Two late cells (**45**) were added on the south side of the great cloister, the first (Cell 22) in the third quarter of the fifteenth century, the second (Cell 23) in the 1520s. Neither had a garden, for there was no space for one, and the very fact that they were built at all indicates the pressure that the house was experiencing for new monks to join the community right up to the suppression. Their planning, however, represents a development from the standard plan seen elsewhere in the great cloister.

Cell 22 was a long, narrow building, built gable-on to the wall of the great cloister and extending up to the north wall of the church. Because the church lay on a lower terrace than the great cloister, the cell was built at first floor level over a cellar entered from the adjacent prior's cell. Its cloister door led into a narrow passage which ran the length of the cell. Immediately inside was the entrance to the living room, with a wall fireplace that matched those of the other monks' cells, and a door opposite led into a latrine. Between the living room and the church wall was the study that was lit by a small window that borrowed light from the church. There may have been another window towards the south end of its east wall. The bedroom was placed on a bridge between the cell and the west wall of the church's north burial chapel, with the oratory contrived in the chapel wall itself with a window overlooking the chapel altar. With the exception of the pre-existing walls that surrounded it on three sides the whole of the cell was timber-framed. There was no work room and no private cloister.

Cell 23 was built by Prior John Wilson in the 1520s and is one of a series of buildings described in his surviving letters to Henry, Lord Clifford who was paying for the work. It was built on the most difficult site imaginable around the north burial chapel of the church. The living room, entered directly by the cloister door without an intervening passage, was only 1.23m wide with a tiny wall fireplace. There was a latrine to the west, created by halving the size of the Cell 22 latrine, and a door in the east wall led to the study at a slightly higher level. The study floor was controlled by the height of the passage below that provided the monks' entrance into their church at the level of the great cloister. Between this room and the north wall of the church, at the same level as the living room, was the bedroom and oratory. So cramped was the space available that the cloister wall was cut back to half its original thickness to provide more space in the study, and the east wall of both study and bedroom was jettied out over the garden in front of the chapter house. This cell was entirely timber-framed apart from the west wall of the passage through the range that was retained from an earlier phase. Despite the difficulties presented by the site, this final cell had the same three-room layout common to all of the monks' cells. As with Cell 22, there was no workroom.

The monks' cells at Mount Grace are probably the best surviving examples of Carthusian planning in fifteenth-century Europe, and they can be compared with surviving and excavated examples on the Continent. Perhaps the closest analogy is the charterhouse of Delft (**46**), more or less contemporary with Mount Grace where excavation by H.H. Vos in 1959 revealed the foundations of 18 cells on three sides of the great cloister. Slightly smaller than the Mount Grace cells at 6.2 x 8m internally, there were three distinct differences. Within, the cell had no entry passage and only two rooms on the ground floor, divided by a substantial wall with a centrally placed door. The dividing wall was sufficiently solid to have been carried up into the upper floor. No trace was recorded of the stair. Outside, there was only a single gallery leading to the latrine, and no 'private cloister'. This model, which is typical of the majority of the surviving late medieval cells in European houses, has a bearing on the interpretation of cells at Beauvale, Coventry, and Sheen.

The Beauvale, Coventry, and Witham cells

Only one cell, Cell 3, was completely excavated at Beauvale in 1908, and it is remarkably similar in its planning to the Mount Grace cells (**37c**). The cell was reduced to low walling, and its windows were restored on the basis of the more complete Mount Grace cells. To what extent the recording reflects the then recently-published (1905) excavation at Mount Grace can only be guessed. There are, however, a number of differences. The cell measured 6.1m² internally with walls 1m thick, and it lay in the south-east corner of a garden some 13.1m². The cloister door was not placed centrally but towards the eastern gable, and it led into a lobby or passage 1.2m wide. The east end of the passage contained the wooden winding stair which led to the first floor. Beyond the passage, the cell was apparently divided into

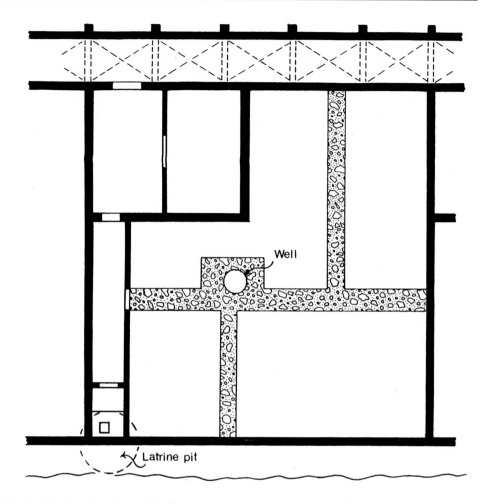

46 *A cell in the charterhouse of Delft*

three rooms on the ground floor by timber partitions set on a stone kerb. The large living room had a tiled floor set a step above the lobby and a wall fireplace. Unusually, the chimney breast of this fireplace projected into the garden of Cell 2. The western part of the cell was divided into two rooms – although the excavators admitted that they did not find any trace of the partition between them – a bedroom and oratory, and a study. Given what happened at Coventry (see below) it is quite possible that this partition did not exist and was simply assumed because that was the situation at Mount Grace. Only re-excavation will determine whether there were three or two rooms at ground floor. Fallen into the cell were the remains of an octagonal chimney with a castellated top, and a gable cross, together with stones from the gable parapets that showed the external appearance of the Beauvale cells to be very similar indeed to those at Mount Grace.

In the garden were two timber-framed galleries set on low stone plinth walls. Both were 1.2m wide. That along the cloister wall was accessed from the lobby of the cell

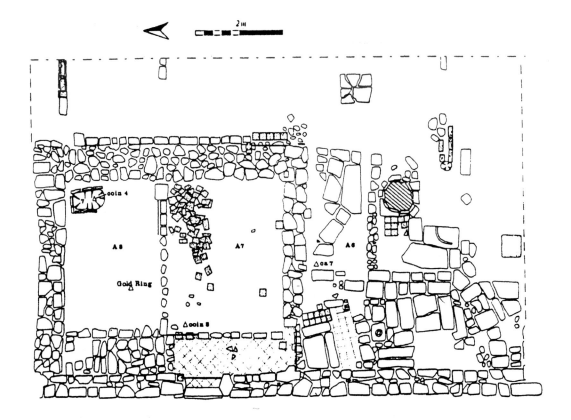

47 *Cell 3 at Coventry*

as at Mount Grace, but unlike those cells a door was provided in the pentice wall to access the garden. The second gallery ran from the back door of the cell in the living room along the garden wall and led to a latrine outside the back wall of the garden. The latrine itself was not found in excavation, only the steps and door leading into it, and the excavators concluded that it must have been timber-framed. They did find the drain it was built over.

At Coventry, we are fortunate in having four cells on the east side of the great cloister which were excavated in 1980-2. These are, in fact, Cells 2-5, known from contemporary documents. Their date is uncertain, but they almost certainly replaced earlier timber cells and are likely to be from the first part of the fifteenth century. All shared a common plan (**37d**), some 6.1m² and set in the corner of a garden plot 10.8m wide and 13.8m deep, with a door placed centrally in their cloister walls. Internally they were divided into a lobby and two rooms on the ground floor, defined by stone kerbs.

Cell 3 was the most completely excavated example (**47**). Immediately inside the cloister door was a lobby 0.8m wide, divided into two parts by a timber partition. The northern half was paved with stone and was probably the site of the stair to the upper floor with a cupboard below it; the southern half was tiled and led to a door in the south wall of the cell, leading to a gallery along the cloister wall. Opposite the cloister door was an entrance into the living room that occupied the southern half of the cell. No trace was found of a fireplace, though there should have been one in the south wall of the cell, but there was a door in the south-east corner of the room that led, unusually, into the garden. A door towards the east end of the partition led from the living room into the northern part of the cell, which the excavator considered to be the bedroom and oratory because it had no external entrance. Normally, there is a door leading to a gallery along the garden wall to a latrine in this location, and this was the case with Cell 2. However, the Coventry cells show a remarkably wide variation in their galleries. In Cell 3, the 1.5m wide gallery on the south side of the cell was not a simple structure. It returned along the south side of the cell and may very well have run around the cell and come back along the garden wall. Unfortunately, the latrines were not examined and their locations can only be presumed.

While the cells themselves had a reasonably common plan, there were slight variations which suggest that they were built one at a time and not as a single building phase. All had tiled lobbies that extended only from the cloister door to the gallery door; had two main rooms on the ground floor, and lay in the north-west corner of their gardens. Three of the four cells excavated devoted more than a third of the entrance lobby to the stair which ran from the northern room and turned against the cloister wall, but in Cell 4 the space usually taken up by the stair was divided into two equal spaces by a partition, leading the excavator to suggest that access to the upper floor must have been by ladder. Flooring also differed; in Cell 2 the living room had a timber floor set on joists, and the other room was tiled. Cell 3 had clay floors in both its rooms while Cell 4 probably had wooden floors, though no joists were traced. The northern room produced evidence of brushwood which had been packed between the joists at Mount Grace to insulate the floors. Against the north wall was a rectangular setting of tiles, suggesting that this was the setting for the hearth of the living room or the location of a bed or piece of furniture. Cell 5 was too badly disturbed to identify its flooring method. Nothing is known of the upper storeys or of the location of the study which is so clearly traced at Mount Grace. Where the ground floor only comprised two rooms the upper storey also may have had two chambers; this was certainly the case at Sheen where several cells survived in recognisable form well into the seventeenth century. A Parliamentary Survey of 1649 mentions 'one other brick tenem(en)t, formerly an Anchorit's cell, cont(aining) two rooms below & two aboue stairs' with a 'long shed', a gallery to the latrine presumably, and a little garden. Considering the northern room of Cell 3 at Coventry had a tile-lined pit in its floor, one of the ground floor rooms may have been the work room, placing the bedroom and oratory and study on the upper floor.

The small scale of the Coventry cells was compensated for in the treatment of the gallery along the cloister wall in Cells 2 and 4. Cell 2 had no 'private cloister' but a room the same depth as the cell itself entered from the lobby of the cell. In its floor were two large tile-filled pits, possibly soakaways, and a substantial drain.

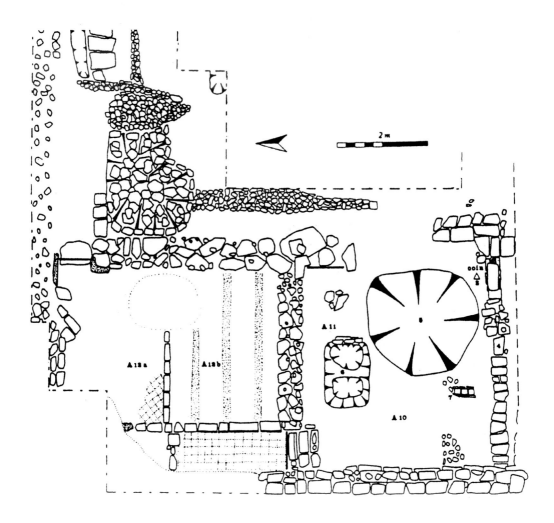

48 *Cell 4 at Coventry*

Whatever was going on here it was not meditation. Cell 4 (**48**) was treated similarly, again with a single storey room slightly narrower than the cell. This room had a tiled floor, and had a well at least 3m deep against its north wall with a drain leading away from it towards the cloister. Some sort of industrial process is likely, though excavation did not identify it.

Only one cell, on the north-west side of the great cloister, is known at Witham, and that was not fully excavated. It lay in the south-eastern corner of its garden and was 5.25m² internally (**37b**). Its walls survived only as footings 1.5m wide, and the linings of its doors had been robbed out. No evidence was found for any internal partitions, fireplace, or stair, but all of these can be presumed. The door to the latrine gallery in the back wall of the cell had been blocked before the suppression and a water tank constructed outside within the gallery. In plan it is closer to Beauvale and Coventry than to Mount Grace and thus probably belongs to the late fourteenth or early fifteenth century.

Gardens

Because every cell had its own garden (until pressure of space in the sixteenth century precluded this at Mount Grace), and the garden was an integral part of the cell, its use was every bit as significant as the individual rooms of the house. Unfortunately, the archaeology of Carthusian gardens, both in England and further afield, has been largely ignored in the study of charterhouses. Mount Grace provides the only evidence in England. Indeed, Laurence Keen's excavation of the gardens of Cells 9 (**colour plate 10**) and 10 was one of the earliest attempts in any monastic context to study the gardens at all. No early gardens have ever been studied.

Hints at what the gardens might have comprised came from Cell 6, where two pottery flower pots (**49**) were found when the garden was levelled for display in the 1960s, before formal excavation was considered. Something similar was found in the garden of Cell 7. Here, three large jugs missing their necks and handles were recovered more or less intact, and it is thought they had been sunk into the garden to contain plants. Nothing, however, is known about the layout of these two gardens, even though excavation has shown that they are in fact capable of demonstrating a variety of layouts every bit as interesting as the cells themselves. The L-shaped garden of Cell 9 (**50**) had been divided into three approximately square beds or knots which were edged with lines of stone marking the borders of grass paths between the beds. There were also raised beds along the west and back walls of the garden and the west wall of the cell itself. No trace of planting within the beds was detected, apart from a circular setting of stones in one corner of the south-western bed, but almost certainly the knots were formally laid out in the form of a contemporary pleasure garden. This garden dates to the early sixteenth century and there is probably an earlier layout below it that has yet to be excavated.

49 *Pottery flower pots from Mount Grace*

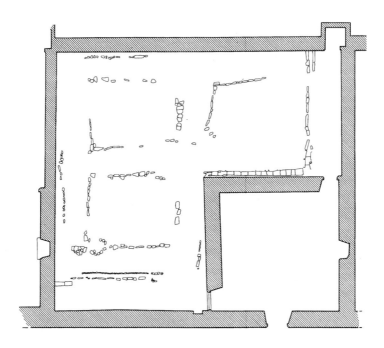

50 *The garden of Cell 9 at Mount Grace*

Cell 10, a corner cell with a larger than average garden, proved to have two phases of development (**51**). The earlier garden, which dated to the early fifteenth century, was defined by rubble-filled slots dug into the natural clay, probably for drainage, outlining a square plot to the north of the cell and two rectangular beds to the west. In the north-western plot a number of pits filled with compost marked the location of the deeper rooted plants, and a further group of planting pits was found to the west of the cell on the east side of an otherwise empty south-western bed. As this plot was the part of the garden entered from the gallery that served as the private cloister, it is tempting to see it as a grassed area with a decorative garden beyond. The north-eastern plot was not excavated to this level because it lay below the only surviving part of the later garden which, dated by finds from the garden soil, belongs to the first quarter of the sixteenth century. It had raised beds that ran along the back wall of the cell, latrine gallery, and back wall of the garden, and was probably little more than an updated version of the original layout. What matters is that it was very different from the contemporary garden of Cell 9; if the internal details of the cells indicated the individuality of their inhabitants, their gardens also demonstrated the monks' personal preferences. Thus while monastic life, particularly that following the rule of St Benedict, set out to suppress individuality in favour of communal spirit, Carthusian life allowed a remarkable level of self-expression within communities of individuals. This is also apparent when we come to examine the contents of individual cells.

If the gardens of Cells 9 and 10 were to stand alone, it might be thought that the later gardens of the order were all decorative, and served as the *hortus inclusus* that

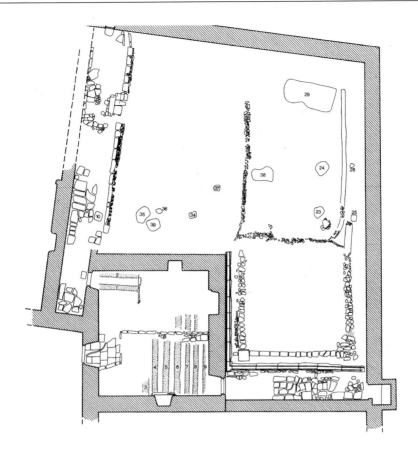

51 *The garden of Cell 10 at Mount Grace*

was an aid to spiritual life. However, they were intended from the first to provide an opportunity for manual labour and for the production of additional food. The excavation of the garden of Cell 8 in 1985 was to show that some gardens might have a more practical application. Its original design (**colour plate 11**) was indeed a *hortus inclusus* with rectangular raised beds separated by paved paths, and with many planting pits and trenches indicating a formalised layout. Soil conditions prevented the recovery of any evidence for what was actually planted, though the compost used in the planting pits and even the ash stakes used to support plants survived in recognisable form. To the west of the cell and in front of the private cloister gallery was a grassed area with a central planting pit that had contained a shrub or small tree staked to keep it upright. Along the cell wall was a slot for a linear planting, perhaps a box hedge. Otherwise this area was featureless apart from the eaves-drip gulley of the gallery roof. To the north of the cell was a large rectangular bed divided into two equal parts by a deep rectangular planting pit and surrounded by paths. Although this area was damaged by later cultivation, both halves of the bed had numerous planting pits, some intercutting to show that there were several phases of planting. Because Cell 8 stood atypically at the centre of its garden, there was a long bed between the cell and its latrine pentice with a series of roughly centrally placed plantings and a trench along the gallery wall that suggested plants grown up the timberwork.

If the late fifteenth-century garden was decorative, what followed it was not. In the early sixteenth century, the raised beds and paths were all swept away, the level of the garden elevated slightly, and new paths which were little more than spreads of burned and crushed sandstone were laid around the three sides of the cell and along the western and perhaps northern walls of the garden (**52**). The monk in this cell was growing vegetables, for along the north side of the cell were a series of narrow V-shaped slots that when first excavated could be seen to have been dug with a round-edged wooden spade. The northern part of the garden at least had been dug in rows. The change from pleasure garden to allotment probably indicates no more than the succession of one monk by another, with a plantsman being replaced by a gardener who was growing vegetables not only for himself but for the community. If all the gardens at Mount Grace were to be examined, it is likely that there would be a mix of garden types, and even some gardens left uncultivated because the monk found his labour in another way.

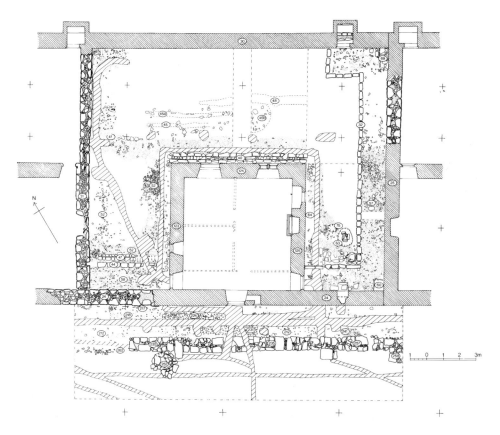

52 *The later garden of Cell 8 at Mount Grace*

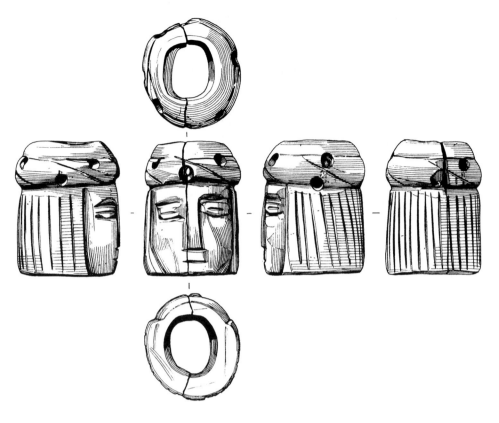

53 *The head of Christ from Mount Grace (actual size)*

The contents of the cells

Because each cell and its garden was enclosed by high walls and rubbish was generally disposed of in the garden, each cell should contain a collection of objects that were used in it and which should provide evidence for the trade practiced by individual members of the community, a situation rarely found on other monastic sites. At Mount Grace, and to a lesser extent at Coventry, this evidence has been examined.

Items associated with spiritual life are extremely rare, but this is probably because they were well cared for, rarely lost, and unlikely to be broken in the normal course of events. Rosary beads are common on most monastic sites, and both Mount Grace and Coventry have produced them in jet. From the prior's cell at Mount Grace, a very rare find was a carved head of Christ in walrus ivory which still retained the pins holes and copper staining of a Crown of Thorns (**53**), again from a rosary. The monks said five of their seven offices in their cells, but some were also charged with prayers for individuals, particularly those buried in the monastic church, and those who had provided money for the monks' prayers, either singly or as a group. The purpose of those prayers is eloquently demonstrated by a small tablet of Caen stone from Normandy found re-used in the floor of the latrine pentice of Cell 10 at Mount

Grace. Below an engraved image of Christ showing the wounds of the crucifixion **(colour plate 12)** is an inscription in English that reads 'the p(ar)don for v p(ater) n(oste)r(s) & v ave(s) ys xxvjM yeres & xxvj daes' (the pardon for five *pater nosters* and five *ave Marias* is 26,000 years and 26 days (spent in Purgatory)). The Carthusians used both Latin and English both in their books and letters, and in their everyday life.

Again at Mount Grace, there are three further devotional objects; cast lead strips **(54)** with the words *Iesus Nazerenus* (Jesus the Nazarene), reversed because they were cast in a positive mould. They come from Cells 10, 11 and 14 and one of the eastern cells of the great cloister (the find spot was not otherwise recorded). What they were used for is far from clear, and it has been suggested that the monks were manufacturing positive impressions from them for sale to pilgrims on the road between the shrines of York and Durham.

We know from Prior Guigues de St-Romain's customs what each cell should have contained, and an analysis of the contents of Cells 2-15 at Mount Grace gives an even clearer picture. Certain things do not survive in the archaeological record either because they were of wood, fabric, or leather and have decayed or because they were of high value like metal vessels and tools and were recovered for scrap or sold off at the suppression. Brother Thomas Golwynne transferred from the charterhouse of London to Mount Grace in 1520 and brought the contents of his cell with him. His prior, William Tynbegh, required a receipt for the goods and although this has not survived the original list has. Apart from two changes of clothes, his blankets, pillows and cushions, Golwynne had a little brass pestle and mortar, five pewter dishes, two tin bottles, one brass chafing dish to reheat his food and a second to heat water, a one-gallon brass pan, a brass skillet with a steel handle, a brass candle stick, a double still for making spirits, and a loom for weaving. None of these items is known from the archaeological record. What is extant, however, is the everyday material, the pottery, the glass, and evidence of the trade that individual monks practised.

The most important group of pottery to be recovered from Mount Grace came from Cell 8 and dated immediately prior to the suppression of the house. Somebody had taken the entire group of pots from the cell outside the back door and thrown them against the house wall. The heap of pottery sherds that resulted comprised no fewer than 44 vessels including one urinal, nine jugs, two jars, two cooking pots, four

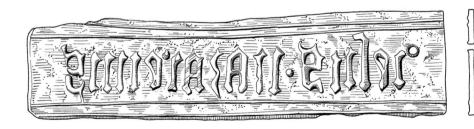

54 *The lead inscription from Mount Grace*

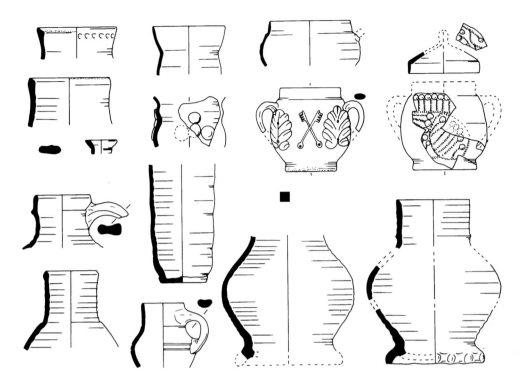

55 *Pottery from Cell 3 at Mount Grace (quarter scale)*

dishes, 18 drinking vessels, an albarello, two drug jars, and a chalice. Why a single monk should require so many pots at one time is unknown, and the quantity of local Cistercian ware cups and German stoneware drinking pots is quite remarkable in any context. Remarkable too is the fact that 20 of the vessels were imports from the Rhineland, the Netherlands, France and Spain. Although plainer vessels were favoured, the quality of the pottery was appropriate to the upper levels of society and we need to remember that Carthusian monks came from the landed classes. Poverty is relative in the monastic world; high quality buildings supported off landed estates imply corporate wealth. Individual members of the community did not technically own anything. By contrast, the charterhouse of Coventry did not produce the quantities of fine tablewares that are apparent in virtually every cell at Mount Grace, leading the excavator to consider that either it was not common in the house or that it had disappeared at the suppression, taken away by the local populace.

Perhaps more typical of a cell assemblage is the pottery recovered from the stripping of Cell 3 in the late 1950s. It comprises many more fragmentary vessels, mainly for drinking (**55**). Almost equal in quantity are the Cistercian ware cups, two with white pipeclay decoration and one with its lid, and the drinking pots from Raeren and Seigberg in Germany. The missing organic component comes from Cell 2 where there were waterlogged deposits; at least three wooden bowls, one with a gothic letter M branded into its base (**56**), and a wooden ladle were found there.

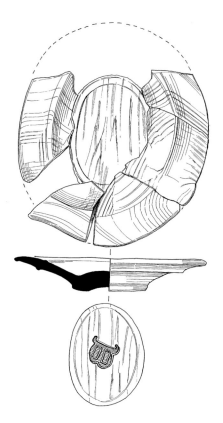

56 *Wooden bowl from Mount Grace*

It is the evidence of trade that is perhaps the most surprising. The principle trade of the Carthusians was the production and copying of books, both for their own use and for others, and Mount Grace has provided remarkable evidence that this was done in a very organised way. The monks in Cells 10 and 11 were both writers, for their cells produced a number of copper alloy pen nibs and Cell 10 additionally contained a lead pencil for lining out parchment pages. If these two monks were the copyists, the monks in Cells 12 and 13 were illuminators, for their cells produced oyster shells with evidence of coloured pigments. The monk in Cell 8 was a book-binder, and the garden and galleries of his cell were scattered with the copper alloy corners, clasps, and studs (some of them unfinished) from the covers of books. It does not take very much imagination to see a lay brother picking up manuscript pages from Cells 10 and 11, taking them to Cells 12 and 13 to have the colour added, and finally taking the finished pages to the monk in Cell 8 where the pages were bound into books. Production on an almost industrial scale was quite possible without the individual monks leaving their cells or meeting each other.

The monk in Cell 10 was not only producing manuscript texts; he also had a stone mould for casting strips of lead type (**57**). This does not necessarily mean he was printing books, though he had the means to do that, but he was certainly dabbling in the latest technology. The most likely suggestion is that he was printing simple

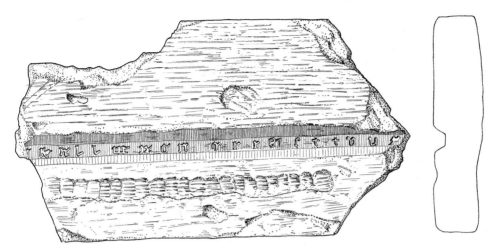

57 *Stone mould for casting metal type from Mount Grace*

things like the certificates of confraternity that other houses like Coventry were selling to their supporters.

Other trades are more difficult to determine. We know that Thomas Golwynne was a weaver. Several members of the community were involved with trade in the widest sense. Coin balances were found in Cells 12 and 14, and official coin weights came from Cell 8 and the cloister alley outside Cell 15, suggesting that individual monks were actually handling cash, something the customs expressly forbade. Thomas Golwynne had a double still and alembic for the production of *aqua vita*, and pottery distilling vessels came from Cells 12 and 20 (a lay brother's cell). These pottery vessels could be used for medicinal or alchemical purposes as well as producing strong drink.

The great cloister

Where other orders used the cloister alleys as their living room, the place where books were copied and read, monks meditated, novices were taught, and the laundry was done and hung out to dry, the Carthusians used them simply as passages between the cells and the church and common offices of the monastery. As a result, the Carthusian great cloister differs in several ways from the cloisters of other monks.

The first thing to notice is its size, which was controlled not by the need to enclose a large area, but because of the need to fit the cells and gardens of the monks around it. Thus the great cloister at Mount Grace was almost twice the size of that at its Cistercian neighbours of Fountains and Rievaulx, even though they were both built for over 100 monks, while at its greatest extent Mount Grace had only 17. The cloister alleys were also narrow, for they did not need space for the community to congregate or desks for study and writing; so those at Witham and Hinton were only

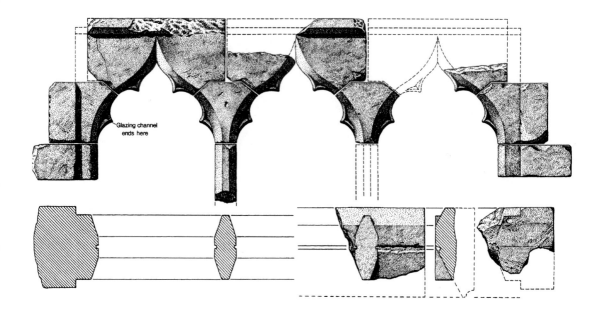

Glazing channel
ends here

58 *The 1420s cloister arcade from Mount Grace*

1.44m wide against the cells, and at Hinton 1.69m wide on the north side against the communal buildings. At Beauvale, the cloister alley was only 1.22m wide where it was excavated outside Cell 3, at London it was 1.25m, while at Axholme it was 2.5m wide on the west side of the great cloister. At Mount Grace, where three sections of the cloister have been excavated, it was found to be 1.95m wide on the north, west, and south sides, and a little wider on the east side where it had been rebuilt in the later fifteenth century. At Mount Grace, the alley had been paved with sandstone slabs which survived only at the south-west corner; at Hinton and London, however, the alleys were tiled. The nature of the floor is not recorded elsewhere.

Only at Mount Grace do we know anything about the superstructure, and that is only because many elements have been discovered in excavation and site clearance. Built in the 1420s, it was an elegant structure (**58**), supported every 6.25m by a shallow buttress. Between each pair of buttresses were two groups of three ogee-headed lights 0.5m wide. Originally, the windows were not glazed, and unlike the majority of larger charterhouse in Europe, the alleys were not covered with a stone vault, but simply by a slated pent roof. Glass windows had been rather clumsily inserted in the last quarter of the fifteenth century. This was not the first cloister alley at Mount Grace; the first had been a simple wooden affair supported on a ground cill, and not all of this had been rebuilt in the 1420s, for a section to the west of Cell 8 survived until the suppression. Obviously it had been rebuilt in sections, and not all of it had been in place when the community began a further rebuilding in the 1470s. Quite clearly, the cloister alley was little more than a covered gallery open to the wind and the rain, though it was built at a time when

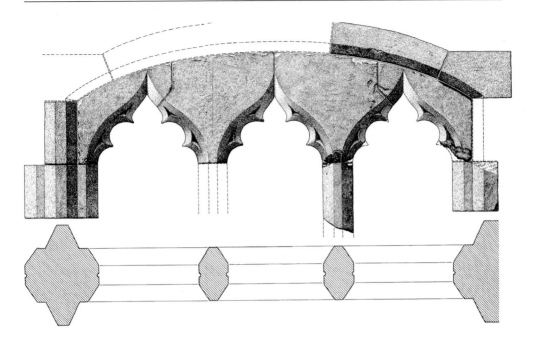

59 *The 1470s cloister arcade at Mount Grace*

other orders were erecting cloister alleys with fine glazed windows, in many cases with desks or carrels for study built into them.

The rebuilding of the cloister at Mount Grace coincided with a period of patronage by Edward IV, and was restricted to the eastern alley which possibly had not been reconstructed in the 1420s but had remained in timber. The alley was slightly widened to a little over 2m, and copied the general form of the earlier stone structure (**59**), though it used a very different technique of building. Again there were two sets of three ogee-headed lights between pairs of deep buttresses, but instead of the windows being set in square-headed recessed panels, the window heads were set below a chamfered segmental arch running from the buttresses to a central mullion that was twice as deep as the mullions that supported the window heads. It was a very substantial structure that suggested both wealth and permanence. This cloister alley was designed to have glass in its windows from the first, and it is significant that the cloister was being glazed at about the same time that glass windows were starting to replace wooden shutters in the cells themselves. The Carthusians were permitting themselves an increasing level of comfort.

The only feature of the Carthusian cloister that is common to the cloisters of other orders was the provision of a *lavatorium* or laver where the monks washed their hands before the meals they ate in the refectory. It was not always in the cloister, for at Coventry its blocked recess can still be seen in the east wall of the prior's house which lay outside the great cloister. At London and Mount Grace, however, it was centrally placed in the south alley, and at Mount Grace it survives, a small laver large enough to be used only by one monk at a time (**colour plate 13**).

Other buildings in the great cloister

There are two buildings which are normally associated with the great cloister; the prison for recalcitrant monks, and the library. Both survive at Mount Grace (**colour plate 14**), though they remain unknown on any other site in England. The prison was one of the earliest buildings to be built and lay at the south-west corner of the great cloister. It comprised two tiny rooms 2.7m², one on top of another; the ground floor room was entered through a very narrow door from the cloister, the upper room by an external stair against the north wall. Both rooms had a latrine on the west side, and the upper room has a small window looking out over the cloister. There was just sufficient room for a bed and a table, and no provision for leaving food and drink such as that seen in the monks' cells. The prison was used to house monks who disturbed the peace of the cloister, broke their vows, or who were shipped from another house as part of their punishment. These men had often broken down mentally from the strain of eremitic life, and probably the worst treatment they could have been given was the close confinement that these two prison cells indicate. They were, however, used for the first 75 years of the house's existence before they were converted for other purposes.

In the 1470s, a new building was added to the north side of the prison linking it to Cell 15 at first floor level. Entered also from the cloister up a narrow stair (using the old prison door which was moved for that purpose), the first floor room was lit by a small traceried window looking out over the cloister. The ground floor chambers were used for storage, but the upper room is almost certainly the convent library which extended into the top prison cell by means of a stair. It replaced the private cloister of the monk in Cell 15 and had a door from his work room. We can assume that this monk was the keeper of the library and it was there that he could read and meditate.

5 The communal buildings

Normally, monks did everything communally, and around their cloisters are placed the common eating hall or refectory, their kitchen, and the house of their abbot or prior. In the inner court which was usually associated with the south and west ranges of the cloister were placed the bakehouse and brewhouse, granaries, stables, accommodation for servants, and lodgings for guests. The Carthusians needed all of these offices and had to fit them in as best they could. The side of the great cloister nearest the church was the usual location for the prior's cell and refectory, though they might be elsewhere; the inner court containing service buildings was invariably associated with these spaces, while guests were accommodated with the lay brethren in the lower house where it existed, and within the inner court where it did not. Where there was no correrie the lay brethren had to be housed as best they could outside the great cloister. All of these buildings are classed as the common buildings of the house.

The prior's cell

The Carthusian prior was appointed to his position of authority by the community, but remained primarily a monk with the same obligations as his brothers. His cell was placed between the great cloister and the inner court because he had responsibilities in each direction; pastoral care for his community as well as the representative it in the wider world. His cell therefore had to combine the spaces needed by a monk with a hall in which he could entertain important visitors.

Three prior's cells survive in England, at Hinton, Coventry and Mount Grace; the latter site actually contains early and later cells that show how the building was developing throughout the fifteenth century. The prior's cell at Hinton is a building of the last two decades of the thirteenth century, and survives almost complete on the north side of the great cloister, below an upper room that is almost certainly the refectory. The close proximity of these two buildings is common and probably originates in the prior using the refectory on occasions as his personal hall, though the custom continued long after he was provided with a hall of his own. Exceptionally, the Hinton cell is vaulted in four double bays, and is divided by a masonry wall into two rooms, one much larger than the other. The western room which is entered from the cloister has a fireplace in the west wall, and must be the prior's living room. A door in the north-west corner led to a latrine in the garden to the rear. The larger eastern room may have been subdivided by timber partitions into two rooms (there are sockets cut into the eastern pillar), and at the west end had a hatch like the monks' cells at London and Mount Grace. A door flanked by blocked windows in the centre of the north led out into the garden behind the cell, and a second door in the south end of the east wall opened into a passage with a stair that led up to the refectory. A blocked recess in the outer face of the east wall marks the site of the cloister laver, and this indicates that the passage had a door into the cloister. If it follows the pattern of Coventry and Mount Grace, this passage was also the main entrance to the cloister, and the prior's cell was placed against it so that he could control access to and from the great cloister.

London poses something of a problem because its prior's cell, which has been partially excavated, was a standard cell identical to those of the other monks, at least in scale and outline. It lay in the south-west corner of the cloister next to the refectory which separated it from the next cell. In this it was similar to the prior's cell at Coventry, which retains some of its features and may cast light on the appearance of the London prior's cell. At Coventry, the prior did not live in the cloister but between the north alley of the cloister and the nave of the church in a long range of buildings on the west side of a lesser cloister. Immediately south of his cell was a passage through the range, probably the entrance from the inner court, and his cell door was in the north wall of the passage. He had no hatch unless it is concealed by modern plaster, and his only door led into what is now a single room 5.8m wide and 8m deep, with a spiral stair in the north-east corner. Originally, there must have been a lobby from the door to the stair, and a single room 5.8m². Unfortunately, the west wall is heavily rebuilt so no trace remains of windows, but unless it was divided by a partition of which no trace now remains this space seems to have been a combined study and bedroom and oratory. The stair led to a substantial upper room 8m² with a large wall fireplace on its east side and a big six-light square-headed window with heavily moulded internal reveals in the east wall. This was the prior's hall, a room of some quality to judge from the carved tie-beams that are all that survives of its medieval roof. It is known that this cell was built at the same time as the refectory to the north by Prior William Solland between 1408–17, and it does not appear to have been altered before the suppression.

The prior of Mount Grace lived at the west end of a range along the south side of the great cloister to the west of the church, with the inner court to its south. Although the location differed from that of Coventry, there were two similarities. The entrance to the cloister was immediately adjacent where it could be controlled directly by the prior, and the refectory occupied the other half of the range. There the similarity ends. Excavation has shown that the prior's cell was built in about 1400, one of the first stone buildings to be erected; surviving masonry shows that it was on two floors; and it is known to have been abandoned for a new site in the late 1420s. It is therefore slightly earlier than its counterpart at Coventry, but was still in use when that building was constructed.

The ground floor of the cell survived almost intact (**colour plate 15**); three rooms separated by wooden partitions on stone cill were all accessed by a tiled corridor that ran from a wider lobby inside the cloister door along the north and west walls to a back door that led to a latrine. A dog-legged food hatch and a niche for a tap were provided in the north cloister wall, indicating that the prior had exactly the same services as other members of his community. Because the building was on a steep slope, the northern corridor was a full metre above the other ground floor rooms and there were steps down into them, though these had not survived later alterations. Internally, the cell measured 10.5m long and 8m wide, with a single upper room of the same size. The location of the stair to the upper room, which was probably a hall as at Coventry, is not known.

The use of the rooms can be determined. In the north-east corner was the prior's bed-chamber and oratory. Having no external walls, it could only be lit by borrowed light from the corridor to the east. It had a door in its south wall leading to a small living room with a fireplace in the south wall of the range. Opposite the fireplace was a long stone bench built against the partition wall. Both of these rooms were found to have mortar floors, possibly the bedding for floor tiles. The western half of the cell comprised a large room with another mortar floor. Lit by windows in the now-missing south wall it was probably the prior's study, the room in which Prior Nicholas Love translated St Bonaventura's 'Mirror of the Life of Christ' into English. Again, it would appear that an effort was being made to provide the prior with accommodation very similar to that of his monks. The only real difference was the upper hall in which he could entertain in the way that his position outside the community demanded.

The migration of the prior to the eastern half of the range in about 1430 provides a good comparison with his original cell and indicates a degree of development which is not seen anywhere else in England. The new cell, built in the shell of the original refectory, was exactly the same size as the original prior's cell, but its layout was very different. The entrance to the new cell was through the old refectory door in the east wall of the corridor that ran through the range, and this led into a living room with a large projecting fireplace in its north wall. Post holes in the floor show that the southern part of the room had been partitioned off to enclose a stair to the upper floor, with its door at the centre of the partition wall. Any windows had to be in the missing south wall of the range and light would be borrowed from the partitioned stair, making this a rather dark room and explaining why there was a candle bracket on either side of the fireplace. A new wall across the range separated this room from a large bedroom and oratory, and a door inserted into the east wall led to a latrine in a small garden to the north of the church. This second room was not divided into two, though there was a small lobby inside the door to the garden, and it would appear that the prior had dispensed with a separate study. The upper floor, lit by the traceried refectory windows of which at least one survived into the sixteenth century, made a very satisfactory hall. Development did not end here, however. By the 1470s, substantial improvements were made to the upper hall and the ground floor was rearranged. The eastern part of the north wall was taken down and rebuilt incorporating a new door and food hatch from the cloister and the base of a fine half-octagonal oriel window looking out over the cloister. The south wall opposite was also widened, probably to support another oriel window looking out over the yard to the west of the church. The prior had abandoned his original door at the west end of his cell because the corridor through the range had been blocked off and converted into a stair up to the replacement refectory. In the 1470s a wide door had been inserted in the north wall of this corridor and it was obviously unsuitable as the entrance to the prior's cell. His hall, however, now stood comparison with those of any other major local landowner, an indication of the raised status of a Carthusian prior at least outside his community. Although the prior remained a monk with all the responsibilities that entailed, he was being required more and more to deal with the outside world on equal terms. All the same, there were clear indications of his spirituality. The oriel window looking over the cloister was screened off from his hall to form a small oratory, and in the living room, a rare find was a carved head of Christ which had fallen from Prior John Wilson's rosary in the 1530s (**53**).

The refectory

Although the Carthusians ate together only on Sundays and major festivals, they still required a refectory like other monks. These survive at Hinton, Coventry, and Mount Grace. In every case, they are associated with a laver, for the Carthusians observed ritual washing before meals.

The Hinton refectory (**60a**) on the top floor of the prior's cell survives with the exception of its upper walls and roof, converted to a granary, a room 14m long and 7m wide. Its original door survives at its north-east corner and the partly-blocked remains of two of its originally three windows look out over the great cloister. The central window has been destroyed by a granary door. Apart from two lancet lights in the west gable wall, the room is featureless.

Early refectories tend to be placed on the first floor, a habit adopted by the Carthusians from the Benedictines but one which also copies the late eleventh- and twelfth-century aristocratic halls of their early patrons. The biblical model was of course the upper room of the Last Supper. Other reforming orders such as the Cluniacs and the Cistercians placed their refectories on the ground floor, a form of humility which allowed them to develop large buildings open to the roof. It was not until the fifteenth century that the Carthusians in England were to move their refectory to the ground floor.

At Coventry (**60b**) the refectory is still at first floor level between the prior's cell and the west end of the church, and it survives almost complete, a building of two bays lit on its east side only by two large windows. Though they have been blocked up, they are large enough to have had elaborate tracery below their four-centred heads. The refectory stands above two service rooms, one of which must have contained the stair up to it. The south wall retains its wall painting, the lower half of a depiction of the Crucifixion that originally extended up into the gable, showing that the refectory was open in the standard English manner to the roof, which here has three finely carved tie-beams that match those in the prior's hall to the south.

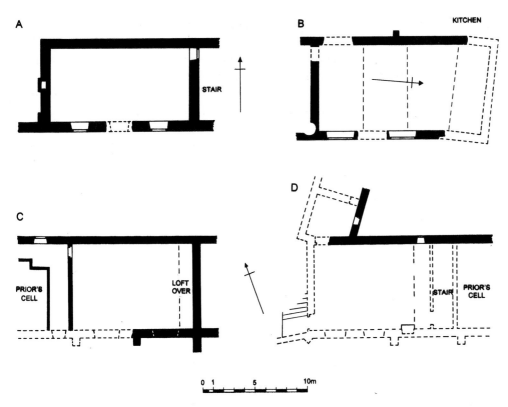

60 *Comparative plans of refectories*

The painting of the Crucifixion on the wall of the refectory was not a Carthusian peculiarity. The Cistercians used the same imagery at Cleeve in the late fifteenth century, and it was seen as a suitable reminder of the monks' daily purpose. At Coventry, it was also used to demonstate patronage; the Roman centurion has a pennant on his lance with the arms of Langley, patrons of the house, and to the left of the cross is a figure of St Anne, the house's patron saint. In a slightly un–Carthusian manner, the painting also carries an inscription recording the completion of the building by Prior William Solland.

Both the Hinton and Coventry refectories have lost all their fittings in their conversions, and they give no indication of how they were used. They do, however, lack one feature that is common to the refectories of other orders; there is no pulpit from which readings were made during meals. Carthusian meals were taken in silence.

At Mount Grace the original refectory (**60c**) was at ground floor level in the same range as the prior's cell, a room 10.5m long and 8m wide, with two large traceried windows high up in its south wall. It was not entered directly from the cloister alley, but through a small and undistinguished door in a corridor that crossed the range. Open to the roof, it was a substantial space, with whitelimed walls and plain glass in its windows. Its floor was of earth, and in the floor which survived across the building there was no evidence whatsoever for the features found in other monastic refectories.

With other orders, benches were placed against the side walls with tables in front of them set into raised platforms or foot-paces, and the prior's table was placed on a raised dais at one end of the room where he could see every member of the community. Nor are there the normal cupboards next to the door to store napkins and towels. The Carthusians simply placed their tables and benches on the floor, and they did not have the expensively tiled or paved floors of other orders. The picture painted by the building at Mount Grace is one of both quality, for it was a fine building, and simplicity, for it was devoid of any decoration. In comparison, the individual monks' cells were elaborate. Their refectory gives every indication that the community regarded eating communally as a penance. In the 1430s, the community gave up their refectory to the prior who moved his cell there, taking over his first floor hall unaltered (**60d**).

If the Carthusian refectory was a simple building, the structures that supported it, the kitchen, bakehouse and brewhouse were not.

The Carthusian kitchen and its offices

Normally, the kitchen was placed next to the refectory in the monastic cloister, and if that was not possible, it adjoined the refectory on the side away from the cloister; and this seems to have been the model followed by the Carthusians from the early thirteenth century if not before. In the fifteenth and sixteenth centuries, however, this was not always the case. The situation is complicated by the fact that the Carthusians were, and remain, strictly vegetarian, though they did provide meat for their guests. This required the provision of two separate kitchens, either on different sites as at London, or side-by-side as at Mount Grace.

The earliest surviving kitchen in England is at Hinton where it lies in the north range of the great cloister to the east of the prior's cell and refectory. There seems to have been a passage between the two buildings that contained the stair up to the refectory. All that is known about this kitchen is that it had a large fireplace in its north wall and that it remained in use from the late thirteenth century up to the 1530s. At Coventry, the kitchen was placed against the north-west corner of the refectory, but it was demolished in the early nineteenth century and nothing is known about it apart from the scar it has left on the refectory wall. London had two kitchens, known from both documents and the 1430s waterworks plan of the monastery: the guest or flesh kitchen, and the convent or fish kitchen. Their names are self-explanatory. The fish kitchen lay on the west side of the little cloister and comprised a suite of three rooms: the kitchen itself, the buttery (which had a water tap), and the larder. A survey of 1539 describes these rooms and their contents. The fish kitchen in addition to its fireplace had three cisterns of lead all in one, a little furnace of brass, a moveable table, and two hanging shelves; the buttery had twelve barrels, great and small cupboards, and a long table as well as several old tables which were stored there; and the larder had fourteen shelves. The meat kitchen, which was located in a building called 'Egypte' (it can be seen on **colour plate 20**) to the south of the church well away from the strictly vege-

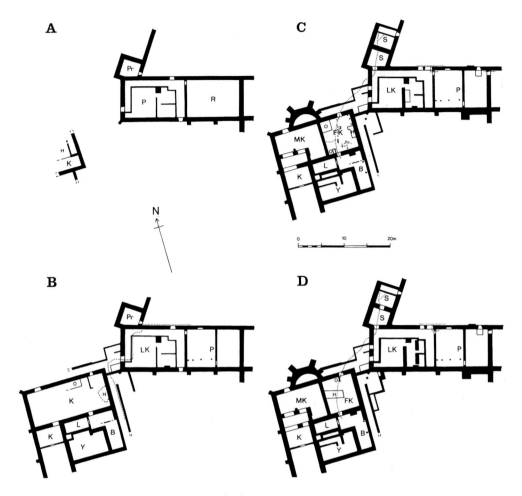

61 *The development of the Mount Grace kitchens*

tarian convent kitchen, was similarly fitted. Neither building has been excavated and their layout is unknown. We have to look to Mount Grace to provide details of the late medieval Carthusian kitchen and its offices.

The arrangements at Mount Grace differ from those at London in that the fish and meat kitchens developed side by side from the 1420s, and were divided by a solid wall from the 1470s. Otherwise, they are remarkably similar to the rooms featured in the London survey. Initially a small kitchen (**61a**) was built a little over 10m to the west of the building that contained the prior's cell and refectory, requiring food to be carried across an open court to the refectory or to the cloister for distribution to the monks' cells. Food can hardly ever have been warm when it was served. In the 1420s however the construction of a new guest house range on the west side of the inner court was combined with a cross-wing at its north end which contained the convent kitchen (**61b**). This comprised a room 17m long and 7m wide, with a battery of ovens along its north wall and an open fire against its east gable. The western half of the building served the guests, but all of its fittings were destroyed in 1901 when that part of the building became a boiler house for the late Victorian residence that was created within the guest lodgings range. The eastern half of the building survived intact in plan, though its walls had been demolished in the sixteenth century. This kitchen served the new refectory on the first floor of the old prior's cell, and the two buildings were linked by a covered gallery that also contained the stair to the refectory. After 20 years, something had finally been done about the food getting cold.

On the south side of the convent kitchen were two rooms, a narrow larder that was probably shelved on both sides like that at London, and an L-shaped buttery that would have stored the beer that was ready for use. As at London, a lead pipe supplied water to the buttery. The kitchen was the preserve of the lay brethren, not the monks, and it was kept in a thoroughly dreadful state throughout the fifteenth century. On the surface of the clay floor was a trampled deposit of coal, charcoal, and ashes from the fire, and vast quantities of fish bones, normally deposited as complete skeletons (**colour plate 17**). When the mess became too unpleasant, normally after about 100mm of trampled fish had built up, a new floor was laid and the process started again. The stench must have been unbearable in the heat of the kitchen. The kitchen was actually too small to serve the convent adequately, and the ground floor rooms of the old prior's cell were converted to serve as a lesser kitchen and store, a use confirmed by the amount of food waste which found its way onto the floors there as well.

In the 1470s (**61c**), the fish kitchen and adjacent meat kitchen were thoroughly remodelled, and a wall built between them. The meat kitchen was given a great chimney with a double fireplace below it (**62**), similar to the great fireplaces of the cloister kitchen of the Cistercians and Benedictines from the twelfth century. It also gained a large oven outside its north wall. The fish kitchen was given a proper hearth of stone and brick for the first time, and the room was divided into two unequal parts by a partition that ran at an angle from the splay of the door in its north wall. In the partitioned space were small ovens set either on a raised bench or built straight onto the floor. South of the fireplace was a bench on which fish were dressed, the many stake holes in front of it being the fixings for duck-boards that avoided the worst of the rotting fish waste on the floor. There was a second table to the north of the hearth, with sockets for its three legs still surviving in the floor. In the sixteenth century, all of this was swept away (**61d**) and the kitchen was provided with an open central hearth.

The Mount Grace kitchen produced some 4 tons of waste material from a period of about 60 years in the fifteenth century. Apart from showing how badly the kitchen was managed, it also gives a fascinating insight into what the monks were actually eating at any particular time. Mount Grace was well supplied with fishponds, yet most of the fish were either marine or were caught in estuarial waters. Before 1450 herring predominated; later it was cod, haddock, and the occasional mackerel against a background of whiting, thornback ray, turbot, flounder, plaice, and sole. There were freshwater and migratory fish, notably carp, which may have been bred locally,

62 *The meat kitchen chimney at Mount Grace*

and eel, with lesser numbers of pike and salmon. A single sturgeon was also noted. The kitchen floor did not simply produce fish, but also copious evidence for shellfish. Again, these varied in different decades of the fifteenth century. Cockles only occurred in the 1420s, though quantities of mussel and oyster were present throughout the use of the kitchen. Eggs were present throughout, but the only evidence for vegetables came from deposits of the 1520s and 30s. Remarkably there were no cereals at all, though conditions for survival were excellent. There was also a total lack of animal bone – with one exception. Six seal bones were found in

SOUTH RANGE OF INNER COURT–GRANARY & KILN HOUSE

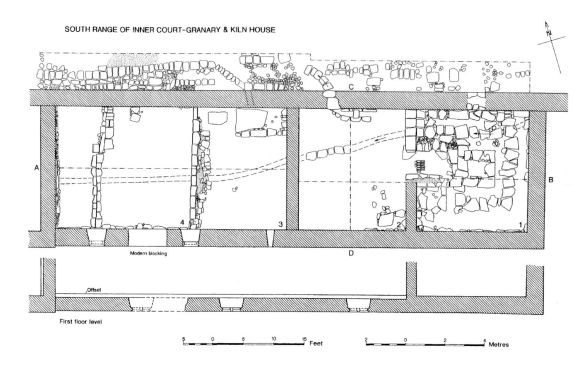

63 *Granaries at Mount Grace*

deposits ranging from the 1430s to the suppression. Clearly, the vegetarian Carthusians regarded seals as fish because they swam in the sea. The products of the convent kitchen would appear to have been an unremitting fish stew or fish pie. The vegetable element of any meal would of course come from the monk's own garden when he ate alone. Communal meals seem to have lacked vegetables.

Coupled with the kitchen and also in the inner court were the bakehouse and brewhouse. No Carthusian examples survive in England, but they must have existed. Each member of the community would have required a loaf of bread and eight pints of ale a day. Similar amounts were allowed for guests and servants. Production of both would have been on a semi-industrial scale. The bakehouse and brewhouse at Mount Grace lay on the east side of the inner court, the only building never to have been excavated. However, the granaries that supplied them survive in the south range of the court (**63**), together with the kiln house in which the barley was malted. The upper section of the entire range comprised granaries, on two floors over the kiln house, a total of 1420m³ of grain storage. Only London and possibly Hull, which bought their bread and beer from local tradesmen, would not have required this sort of provision. It is not clear if those houses with correries had bakehouses and brewhouses in both institutions, though the likelihood is that they were provided only in the lower house because their running was the responsibility of lay brethren or servants.

Guest accommodation

Those orders which followed the Rule of St Benedict accepted a responsibility for the entertainment of travellers and the relief of the poor that was exemplary, and involved the development of substantial guest houses and almonries. The Carthusians in contrast did not actively encourage guests. Prior Guigues of the Grande Chartreuse went so far in his *Constitutions* of the order as to discourage the presence of seculars whose upkeep might force the religious themselves to have to beg alms to support them. If guests chose to stay at a charterhouse they would not be turned away, but would be restricted to the correrie with the lay brethren where they might enjoy no higher a standard of food or bed than the monks themselves. Their horses would not be stabled, even in winter. Religious visitors would be accommodated in the upper house, but again, their living would be the same as an ordinary member of the community, even if they were bishops. Because the correries of Witham and Hinton have never been examined, we know nothing of early guest provision in England. We do not possess a great deal of evidence about guest accommodation in later houses either, with the single and perhaps exceptional example at Mount Grace. This lay on the pilgrimage route between York and Durham, a day's ride from York, and the temptation to cash in on this passing trade appears to have been too great to ignore in the long term.

The guest range at Mount Grace was built in the 1420s on the west side of the inner court just inside the gate (**64**), and it survives largely intact within a house of

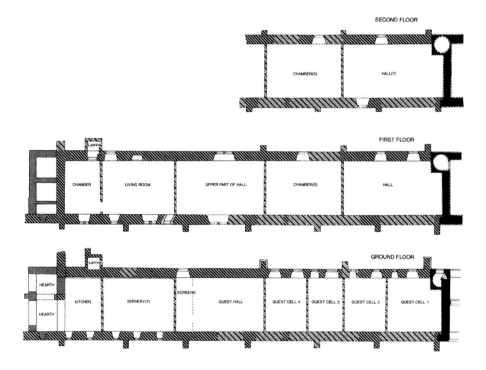

64 *The Mount Grace guest house range*

65 *The second guest house at Mount Grace*

1654 and 1900-1. It is very different from the normal form of monastic guest house which provided high status accommodation and appears to respect the early Carthusian constitutions. The building is divided into three parts; accommodation to the south, an open hall at the centre, and the kitchen and procurator's living area at the north end. The accommodation is simple; four cells on the ground floor with a door and a square-headed window looking into the inner court. No windows survive in the outer wall, which enclosed the inner court. Each guest was thus provided with a private room which was no better than the accommodation of the monks. There was no fireplace and no latrine. Above these four units was a suite of rooms on two floors which was entered from the inner court by a stair, providing high status accommodation. Both side walls in these rooms had windows, all of which had two lights. The accommodation was no better, however, than that enjoyed by the prior, and again lacked any evidence of a fire or latrine. The guest hall was small and inaccessible from the chambers. It was entered through a screens passage at its north end, and lit by large four-light windows in its side walls. Again, there is no evidence for a wall fireplace, though there could have been a central hearth. The only fireplace in the entire building was in the procurator's hall on the first floor at the north end of the building, and here too was the only latrine. Although the building itself was of high quality it cannot be described as comfortable.

If this was the only guest accommodation at Mount Grace, it might be seen as typical of the Carthusian approach to guests. In the 1470s, however, a second guest house was provided to the south of the inner court gate (**65**). On the ground floor were four chambers with a door and a single window to the inner court, again without fireplace or latrine, doubling the original provision. The first floor comprised a common dormitory entered by a door at the centre of its west wall, from the outer rather than the inner court. There was a second floor in the roof space, probably also dormitory space and potentially lit by dormer windows. Guests were obviously segregated by quality, as they were in other monasteries, but it is the number of less wealthy guests which is exceptional. Other orders would have provided an almonry for poorer visitors but there is no evidence that the Carthusians did this. This was not the end of the story, however, for Prior John Wilson records a further building in the outer court known simply as 'le Inne', built by Sir John Rawson, Master of St John's Commandery of the Knights Hospitlar at Swingfield in Kent before he left England in 1521 for the defence of Rhodes. Rawson was one of Brother Thomas Golwynne's sponsors, which explains his connection with Mount Grace. Why Mount Grace should require yet more guest accommodation, what its form was and precisely where it was located, are all unknown.

Lay brethren

Up to the foundation of Beauvale, lay brethren were accommodated in the correrie or lower house. At Beauvale, the excavators speculated that the long range to the south of the church might have comprised their communal accommodation. The range, however, was not excavated and this has to remain supposition. At London Grimes, following documentary evidence, placed them in the ranges to the west of the little cloister, again presuming that their accommodation was communal. Lack of excavation there means that again we cannot be certain. At Coventry, Soden thought that a range of buildings on the north-west side of the church might house the lay brethren, though incomplete excavation there makes this only a possibility. At Mount Grace, however, the six cells of the lay brethren present in 1539 can be identified in a lesser cloister to the east and south of the church. Though five of these cells were laid out in the 1420s or 30s, they were not built in stone until the 1470s, and they share many of the features of the monks' cells. The point at which lay brethren moved from communal to segregated living is not known, though there is no sign at Mount Grace that they ever had communal buildings.

The Mount Grace lay brethren' cells take two forms. The earliest, Cells 20 and 21 (**66**) are rectangular and semi-detached. Cell 21 retains the evidence of its internal partitioning. It was entered through a corridor that ran the length of its west wall and had three rooms; a living room with a projecting fireplace at the north end, a central room of uncertain use, and a bedroom at the south end with a door leading into the garden (which was later blocked up). The latrine lay in the corner of the garden at the end of a gallery entered from the entry passage. There was no evidence of a stair at the south end of the passage and it is assumed that the cells were of a single storey, for the lay brethren, who worked in the common offices of the house, had no need

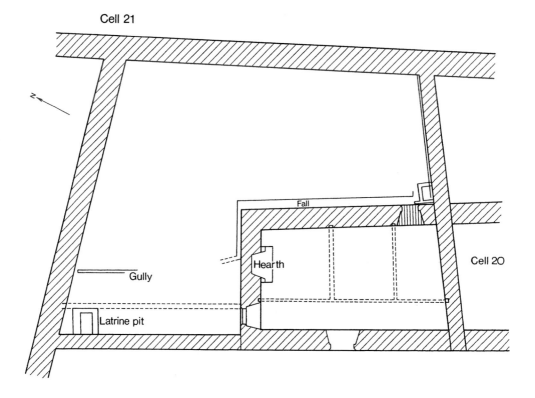

66 *Cell 21 at Mount Grace*

of a work room. Cell 20 was a mirror-image of Cell 21, though it was poorly preserved. It is exceptional because a large group of pottery was recovered when this cell was cleared for display (**67**) which, although it lacks a proper archaeological context, is very informative. This lay brother was using a collection of pottery that was indistinguishable from that used by the monks in the great cloister, with the usual urinal, storage vessels, and the ubiquitous drinking pots from Seigberg and Raeren in the Rhineland.

The second cell-form is best seen in Cell 18 (**68**). This was even closer in planning to the monks' cells, with an entry passage and two rooms indicated by the sockets for partitions. The same projecting fireplace seen in Cell 21 was present here, showing that the western room was the living room, and a latrine in the garden wall indicates a door at the west end of the south wall and a gallery along the side wall of the garden. A second gallery along the wall of the lesser cloister is indicated by a door at the end of the entrance passage, and a large window in the east wall of the eastern room is evidenced by a recess in the wall itself. If there had been a stair to an upper floor it would have been at the west end of the entry passage. Three joist sockets in the cell wall indicated that the floor here was raised above the general level of the passage, precluding the fitting of a stair. All of the lay brethren' cells were excavated in the late nineteenth century, and we know very little about them apart from the

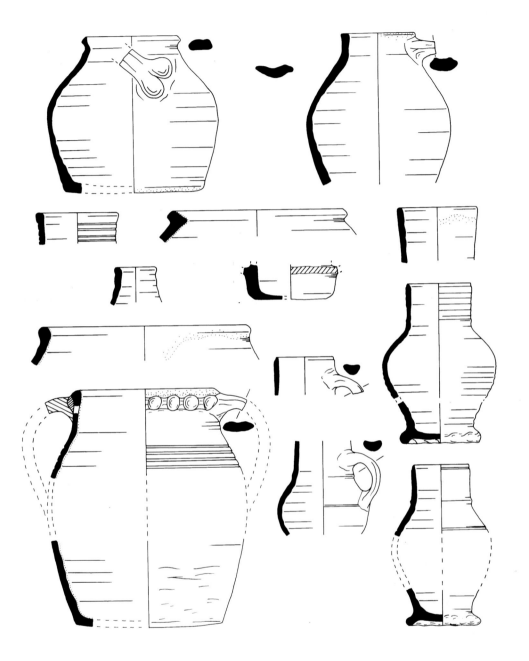

67 *Pottery from Cell 20 at Mount Grace (quarter scale)*

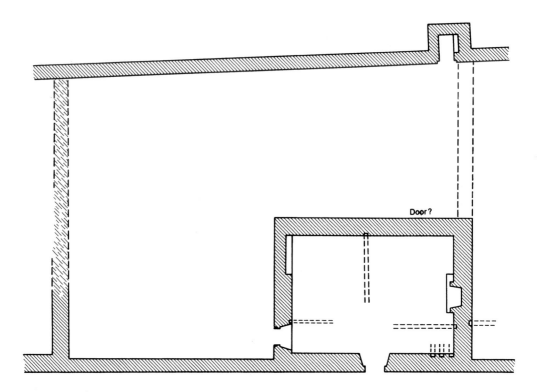

Door?

68 *Cell 18 at Mount Grace*

evidence of their structure. They remain unique in England, and if there is one aspect of Carthusian life that demands further research it is how the lay brethren differed in their daily life from the choir monks they served.

6 The Carthusians and water

Monasteries required copious quantities of water, something that was not always apparent to founders who wanted them to be built near to their castles, on the site of earlier Saxon monasteries, or in some other location with religious associations. Three sources of water were needed: one to drive mills and service the buildings and fish ponds of the outer court, another to flush drains, and a third for washing, cooking, and the making of beer. The first two could be found in rivers and streams, the third had to be engineered, often from a distant source. The Carthusians, though they actively sought secluded sites, were no different to other monks when it came to water though their uses of it were slightly different.

In the earlier charterhouses of Witham and Hinton elevated sites above the River Frome were chosen, but both were close to a river which could be dammed to drive mills and feed fishponds, and at Witham, the evidence for this survives on both the Frome and a tributary (**10**). Later sites were not able to chose so carefully, for all the best locations had long gone. Beauvale and Coventry were probably the last monasteries to benefit from a site that provided all the water they needed. For the later houses, there were other considerations. London was to be founded on a plague cemetery site, and supplanted a college of much smaller scale; at Hull the Carthusians were to inherit a site intended for Franciscan nuns; Axholme was to be centred on a pre-existing chapel in the woods at Owston Ferry; and Sheen was to be built next door to the royal palace of Richmond. Mount Grace was to occupy the site of a pre-existing village nearly a mile from the River Wiske. If a convenient water supply did not exist, there was the technology available to create one.

Potable water

The Carthusians alone of the monastic orders in England drank water on their fast days as opposed to the ale that was the common drink. Drinking water in the Middle Ages was a fairly unhealthy experience at the best of times, and its conversion to ale at least required it to be boiled. Though the process of purification was not understood, the cleaning and filtering of potable water was introduced into England by Henry of Blois, Bishop of Winchester at his palace of Wolvesey in the 1130s. By the 1160s, when a distant water source was relayed via conduits by Canterbury cathedral priory, a sophisticated array of settling tanks and filter beds was included to ensure that the spring water brought in to the precinct was clean. The Benedictines used

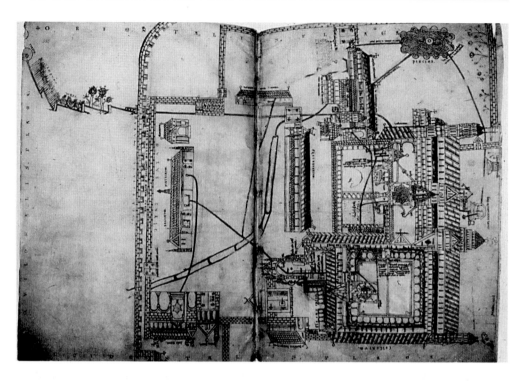

69 *The water supply of Canterbury cathedral priory is clearly defined on a contemporary plan drawn in the 1160s.* Trinity College, Cambridge

the water for ritual washing at lavers in the infirmary, infirmary cloister, and main cloister before the recycled water got to the kitchen, and only after it had left the kitchen did it go to the brewhouse (**69**). The cleaning of this water was primarily spiritual; it was not intended to be drunk.

Water supply in the London charterhouse

The original supply of the London Carthusians is not known, and it may have originally had to use wells on its own site. The charterhouse was given a spring on the manor of Barnersbury in Islington in 1430, 59 years after the foundation of the monastery, and from here constructed a fully-engineered water supply to the monastery over a distance of some two miles. This in itself was not unusual and two other London monasteries, the great hospital-priory of St John of Jerusalem and the Augustinian nuns of Clerkenwell, also took their water from this area. What is remarkable is that a contemporary plan of the Carthusians' water supply exists (**colour plates 17, 18, 19 & 20**), together with a copy made after 1512, which details how the supply was engineered and modified throughout the life of the charterhouse. Such is the detail of these plans that it is possible to see exactly how the system was organised. Originally four springs, later increased to eight, were tapped and well-houses built over them, and the water was led in a stone channel to a conduit house or 'howse of recete' which survived in modified form until 1831 as the White Conduit in Denmark Road, Islington. The conduit house was a rectangular building divided into two unequal parts: the northern end contained a cistern into which the water discharged through a lead pipe with a perforated rose on the end of it. An overflow pipe controlled the height of the water and led away any surplus, and a second pipe with a rose took the water from the reservoir towards the charterhouse. Entering into the land of St John of Jerusalem, which the piped crossed by licence, two further springs were tapped and the pipe entered a small stone building which is labelled the 'first wind vent' which controlled the pressure in the pipe. As it crossed the field called Commanders Mantel belonging to St John's, the supply pipe ran through three 'wells', probably settling tanks, square buildings lined with lead. A single pipe entered the first, but two pipes left it. At the second 'well' the supply pipe was tripled as it ran towards the second conduit house on the system, a large brick building with a lead roof. It was vaulted inside and contained a large tank that filled the whole building, and into which the three incoming pipes discharged. The building is drawn in incredible detail. In the base of the tank was a plug which could be withdrawn to drain it off; the height of water was controlled by an overflow pipe which led waste water into a stone gutter which ran off in the direction of St John's own conduit house in the same field; and a massive pipe in the south wall took the supply off to the charterhouse. This pipe, the 'home pipe' had two features associated with it. Where it crossed the road from Islington to London and entered the field of the nuns of Clerkenwell there was a 'suspiral' or air vent, and where it entered into the charterhouse land a pipe is taken off the home pipe to a tank on the edge of the ditch that divided the Carthusians' land from a field belonging to St John's that was called a 'spurgell'. This was designed to drain off the charterhouse water system when it was cleansed or repaired. The system was a relatively simple one using technology which had been available since the middle years of the twelfth century, closely comparable to the system installed by Prior Wybert at Canterbury in the 1160s (**69**).

Within the charterhouse, the plumbing is peculiarly Carthusian. The home pipe ran to the centre of the great cloister where there was a water tower or 'age', a stone octagonal structure with a jettied upper storey if timber. The upper storey contained a tank into which the water ran under pressure, and from here lead pipes ran to each side of the great cloister and branched off to serve individual cells. On each branch there was a suspiral to reduce the pressure, small tanks within the cloister garden. Thus, the cells of the west, north, and east sides of the great cloister received their water directly from the water tower, clean and potable. In the south range, something different happened. The water was taken first to the cloister laver as would normally happen in the houses of other orders, and water from the laver was piped to the three cells at the east end of that range, the laundry, the kitchen and buttery, the brewhouse, and the meat kitchen. The cells of the south range were the last to be built, and their supply must post-date the original arrangement. The sacrist, whose cell was next to the chapter house, had two taps, one in his cell which is not labelled on the drawing, and another which is labelled 'the sexten is cook in hys wassynge place'. Washing, probably of the liturgical vessels in the sacrist's keeping, was clearly separated from water which could be drunk.

70 *The northern well house at Mount Grace*

The supply of water at Mount Grace

Because Mount Grace was established on a natural spring-line there was no need to engineer a supply of clean water from a distance. It simply bubbled out of the hillside and could be collected in well-houses. Mount Grace had not one well-house but three, which served three distinct parts of the house. That on the north (**70**), the largest and most complex, served the great cloister; the central one (**71**) supplied the lesser cloister, and the third to the south provided water to the inner court. This well-house, known as St John's Well (**72**), remained in use until 1901, leading water to a seventeenth-century house built in the ruins of the guest house range. The springs did not rise in the well-houses but into tanks in the hillside behind them, and ran in stone gutters reminiscent of London into the well-houses through holes in their back walls. Each well-house contained a lead tank which was effectively a settling tank, for a pipe was taken out from the top as opposed to the bottom, allowing sediment to be separated from the water that was used. The northern well-house is the most complete, and the stone channel in which its outlet pipe ran remains below the paving in front of it. This pipe ran across the garden of Cell 4 in the east range, below the eastern cloister alley, and towards the centre of the great cloister in a stone channel that protected it from disturbance. The pipes from the other well-houses have not been traced.

71 *The central well house at Mount Grace*

72 *St John's well, south Mount Grace well house in 1900*

Mount Grace had a water tower at the centre of its great cloister similar to that at London, and since it has been excavated twice, once in 1900 and again in 1988 (**colour plate 21**), its form can be reconstructed with some confidence. Unlike the London water tower which was some 20m lower than its water source and could be filled by pressure, the tank at Mount Grace was at almost the same height as the well-house that supplied it and water had to be pumped up. The site of the pump, an area of pitched paving next to a drain which carried off waste water, remained on the east side of the tower and the course of the supply pipe could be traced towards it. The tower itself had been destroyed in the sixteenth century, though fragments were recovered in 1900, and all that remained where the piles on which it stood. These showed that it was about 2m in diameter, and stood exactly in the centre of the garth (**73**). When Sir William St John Hope excavated it, he noted that it was an octagonal structure with buttresses at the angles, similar to that at London. It was in fact very much more elaborate, with paired windows in each face, which excavation revealed had been filled with coloured glass. No trace was found of its upper storey, which must have been of timber like the London water-tower. Unfortunately gardening

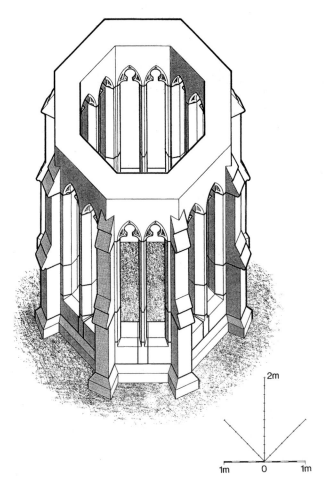

73 *Reconstruction of the lower storey of the Mount Grace water tower.* Simon Hayfield

74 *The tap niche in Cell in Cell 6 at Mount Grace*

since the seventeenth century had removed any evidence of the pipes that ran from the water tower to the cells of the great cloister, and it can only be supposed that a system similar to London was used.

A ring-main ran around all four sides of the great cloister below the floors of the alleys, close to the cell walls, and parts of the pipe still remain in place. At each cell, a spur was taken off the main, through the wall of the cell or its garden, to a tap which was placed in a simple niche (**74**) just above floor level. No taps have survived but the impression of the pipe remains in almost every case.

Potable water in other Carthusian houses

Although London and Mount Grace provide exceptional evidence for piped water, they are not alone. At Hinton, excavation has revealed slight evidence for lead water-pipes associated with the cells, though this was not recorded by the excavators because the pipes had been withdrawn at the suppression. What remained were the carefully-cut channels in which the pipes had run, and these were mistaken for drains. Geophysical survey at both Witham and Hinton failed to find any trace of a water-tower at the centre of the great cloister, and it may very well be the case that this was a late medieval development. At Beauvale, however, a water-tower and the pipe runs associated with it were located in the great cloister (**colour plate 22**), and the excavators found evidence very similar to that at Mount Grace for a ring main running around the cloister and spurs leading to Cells 2 and 3 on the north side. The situation at Axholme remains uncertain because of the degree of post-suppression remodelling.

London was not the only charterhouse to have a distant water supply. When Henry IV established the charterhouse of Sheen next to his palace he gave the community the spring of Hillesdonwell. This must have proved inadequate because Edward IV added the source of Welway or Pickwelleswell, with permission to build an underground conduit. The system was still functioning in the mid-seventeenth century, when lead pipes and brass taps are recorded in the cells that had been converted to houses after the suppression. What happened at Hull and Coventry is quite unknown, but the likelihood is that they followed the same model as Mount Grace and London. As with the development of cells, it would seem that there are 'early' and 'late' hydraulic systems.

Water for drainage and industry

Potable water was always separate from that used to service the latrines, mills, and fishponds, and this was as true of the Carthusians as it was of other monastic orders. Witham and Hinton, functioning with correries on the River Frome, were able to separate their water supplies by function in a much clearer way than is apparent in the later houses of the order in England. Only at Mount Grace is it known how the service water supply worked, the result of a major landscape study undertaken in the 1980s.

Mount Grace was built on a natural perched terrace below the scarp of the North Yorkshire Moors. Before it was built, the hillside was scored by surface water run-off channels that had eventually formed three streams and their catchment areas (**75a**). There had been sufficient water to support a medieval village on the terrace, though it was hardly enough to support even a small monastery. The levelling of the site for the charterhouse disrupted all three streams, and part of the initial building was to divert them away from what was to be a building site for the next 30 years (**75b**). New water systems then had to be engineered, for the new community would need to have four separate supplies of water: a clean source for drinking, one to flush foul drains, another to feed a series of fishponds, and a fourth to drive their mill. The streams of the central catchment area were utilised to supply water to three well-houses on the hillside above the priory, from which a continuous supply of clean water could be distributed to the house, a close source which was unusual in its simplicity, suggesting that this was the primary reason why the site was chosen in the first place. The stream of the northern catchment was diverted around the north side of the house to feed a series of fishponds on the lower terrace, again a simple operation. The larger southern catchment, however, was substantially modified to bring a water supply into a perched leat on the edge of the main terrace to power a watermill. It was insufficient in itself to drive even a small mill, and additional water had to be found. The nearest source

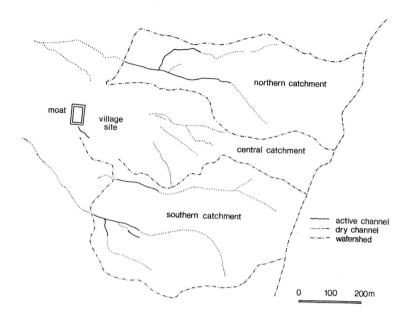

A. SURFACE DRAINAGE IN 1398

northern catchment

moat

village
site

central catchment

southern catchment

—— active channel
········· dry channel
—·—· watershed

0   100   200m

B. SURFACE DRAINAGE IN 1539

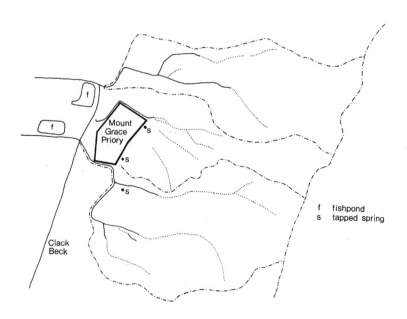

f

f

Mount
Grace
Priory

•s

•s

•s

f   fishpond
s   tapped spring

Clack
Beck

75 *The natural and modified drainage of Mount Grace*

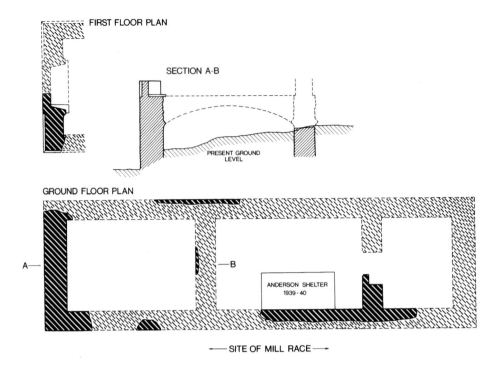

FIRST FLOOR PLAN

SECTION A-B

PRESENT GROUND
LEVEL

GROUND FLOOR PLAN

A

B

ANDERSON SHELTER
1939 - 40

——— SITE OF MILL RACE ———

76 *The Mount Grace water mill*

was the Clack Beck, over a mile to the south of the monastery, and this was diverted in a contour leat to join the stream in the southern catchment to the west of the house. When the mill was not working, the water of the Clack Beck and the southern catchment could be diverted along a new channel that ran away to the west along the access track to the house, and when the mill was working, waste water ran into the diverted stream of the northern catchment and ran away again to the west. By this means, a sufficient head of water was always available for milling. The Clack Beck still runs in its early fifteenth-century channel and first overflow, a tribute to the Carthusians' water engineering. The mill (**76**) still stands on the west side of the leat, a building of the early fifteenth century, indicating that the water engineering all took place in the early years of the charterhouse's life.

Foul drainage in a Carthusian monastery was much more complicated than the great communal systems of other orders, simply because every cell needed its own drainage and because the Carthusians of Mount Grace chose to have a water-flushed system. The same was true of both Hinton and Beauvale. Given the limited local water supply, every last drop of water had to be used. The levelling of the great cloister terrace had uncovered a number of springs, and these were enclosed in stone and the water channelled into stone-lined sewers into which the latrines of the earliest cells drained (**77**). Even the water off the roofs was collected, and transferred into the sewers through a complicated series of drains. Because the sewers were sealed by the levelling material of the great cloister it is clear that they were planned from the first (**78**). Indeed, the

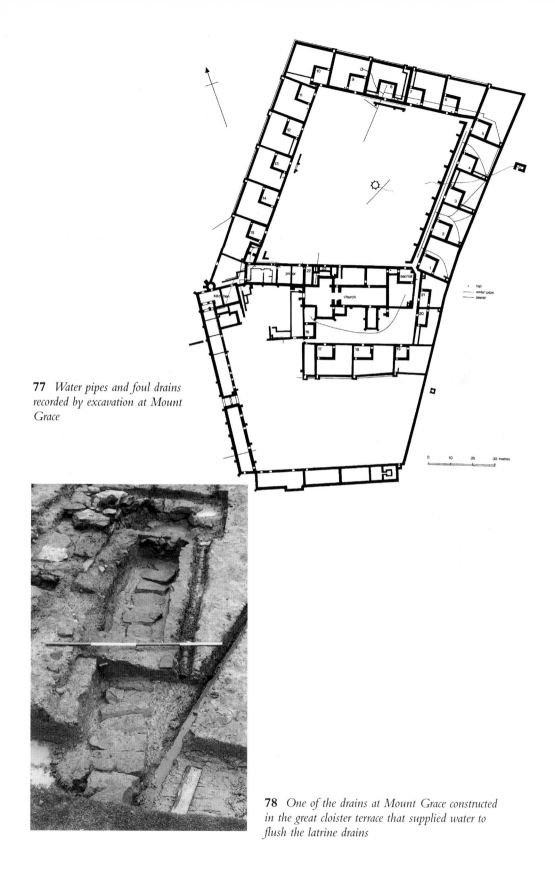

77 *Water pipes and foul drains recorded by excavation at Mount Grace*

78 *One of the drains at Mount Grace constructed in the great cloister terrace that supplied water to flush the latrine drains*

79 *The sewer that served the latrines on the north side of the great cloister at Mount Grace*

sewer that runs from below Cell 8 across the great cloister flows beneath the church, where it meets a second sewer that ran down the east cloister alley before they both turn to the west and discharge into the mill leat. They must have been laid before the church was actually built, though they were constantly being remodelled up until the 1530s. One of the problems with deeply buried sewers is that they had a tendency to block up, presumably in times of drought, and a number of holes had to be dug from the surface to clear blockages. It comes as no surprise that in the 1420s and 30s, when the cells on the north and west sides of the cloister were rebuilt, that it was decided to place the sewer outside the garden wall and not below buildings (**79**). Again, it is a tribute to the original builders that these drains are still running, draining the site of surface water.

7 The suppression and after

Although the later middle ages had seen a general reawakening of piety and an increased interest in monastic life, with most orders seeing a modest growth, there was a growing awareness that many monasteries were no longer properly serving the purpose for which they had been created. The lofty communal ideals of the twelfth and thirteenth centuries had already broken down as monastic life developed; with the creation of households centred on the senior officers of some monasteries, discipline, always a problem but one which increased in the fourteenth and fifteenth centuries, became difficult to enforce; and people seriously started to question how relevant the monastic church actually was. Generally speaking, the growth in the perceived importance of abbots and priors, substantial landowners on behalf of their communities, matched the decline in the outside world's perception of monastic life. Remarkably the Carthusians were able to stand above this, remaining true to their earliest principles, and it was this which led to their ultimate destruction in England.

Early sixteenth-century Carthusian life

A remarkable series of letters written by Prior John Wilson of Mount Grace has survived from the early sixteenth century. Written to Henry, Lord Clifford, who as a major patron of the house was buying land for the monastery and paying for new buildings, these letters indicate that not only did Mount Grace have a full complement of monks and lay brethren and was keeping its buildings in good repair, but there was actually a waiting list of entrants. All of this suggests a thriving community. Wilson's predecessor as prior, Robert Norton, had written to Clifford in 1521 saying that he had workmen in every corner of the monastery and that he needed to buy lead for three cells that had to be re-slated before winter. He was also buying wainscot for the cells, and there was obviously a major refit in progress, one which has in fact left traces in the site's archaeology. In December of the following year, Prior Wilson was quarrying stone for new buildings and for new garden walls. In 1523 one cell was in need of repair, and another almost completed. A third, probably Cell 23, was being built in March of that year, and Wilson had procured the stone, but was having problems in persuading his tenants to lend their oxen to drag it down from the quarry where it was worked because the way was steep and very boggy. Reluctantly he was forced to use the house's own cattle. At the same time, he was trying to dissuade Henry Clifford's chaplain from becoming a Carthusian, pointing out how strict the life was and how difficult the transition from the world outside the monastery.

Because of the Carthusians' natural introspection it is difficult either to reconstruct their lives in the early sixteenth century from their writings, or to interpret it from the mass of propaganda put out by the government in the early 1530s when it took on the Carthusians, the only monastic order to question seriously Henry VIII's ideas on church reform. Archaeology, however, gives us a remarkably clear impression of how Carthusian life was lived at both Coventry and Mount Grace, respectively a fairly poor suburban and a well-endowed rural house of the order. From this, it is possible to see how the historical evidence should be read.

At both Mount Grace and Coventry we have excavated cells that contain finds relating to their latest use and which indicate the standard of life enjoyed by ordinary members of the community. The fact that the cells at Coventry were smaller than those at Mount Grace is perhaps an indicator of the relative wealth of the two foundations, but their structures show that in both cases well-appointed houses were provided and that they were kept in good repair to the very end. Documentary evidence suggests that the same was true of London and Sheen, and that cells there survived the closure of the monasteries to serve as houses for new occupants. The material culture of Mount Grace and Coventry differed, but again that was a sign of their different incomes. What is significant is that cells in the two monasteries contained the same range of pottery vessels, though while Mount Grace enjoyed the use of imported and exotic pottery Coventry made do with predominantly local products. In both cases, the cells had been stripped of anything saleable before they were unroofed, and only a hint of their contents remained. At Mount Grace, we know that many of the monks were working as copyists, their cells containing pens, ink pots, paint palettes and the other debris of writing; we also know from the remains of their library what they were reading and writing. Mount Grace had two exceptional scholars in the early sixteenth century, Richard Methley and Prior Robert Norton, and from their books we know that Mount Grace was at the forefront of modern European devotion and spirituality. They wrote both in Latin and English, for a monastic and non-monastic audience, and they read widely. Mount Grace even had a number of printed books in its library, a sure sign that the community was keeping itself up to date. The impression given by Mount Grace is that the monks were provided with everything they needed to encourage scholarship and religious life.

Similarly, the London charterhouse went through a period of renewal in the early sixteenth century under two of its last three priors: William Tynbygh and John Houghton. Tybygh encouraged exceptional scholars to enter his house, and even accommodated Sir Thomas More within the precinct for four years. It was Prior Tynbygh who renewed and extended the piped water supply in 1512, began the upgrading of its accommodation and oversaw the last extensions to the church. John Houghton joined the community in 1515, became sacrist in 1522, and procurator in 1527. A law graduate from Cambridge who had entered the priesthood he was clearly being trained for the priorate and was dispatched to become prior of Beauvale in 1530. In 1531 he was recalled to London as prior there, where he continued to build his house's reputation. He was replaced at Beauvale with another London monk who had been professed by William Tynbygh, Robert Laurence.

The renaissance seen at London was paralleled elsewhere. Augustine Webster, another Cambridge graduate and a monk of Sheen, was despatched to become prior of Axholme. Together, Priors Houghton, Laurence, and Webster were to bring about the demise of the order in England as they confronted Henry VIII's seizure of the headship of the church in England.

The beginning of the end

The Carthusians came to grief over the Act of Succession of 1534, whereby all the king's subjects were obliged to swear an oath before commissioners that they would recognise the invalidity of the king's marriage to Katherine of Aragon and declare the issue of his second wife, Ann Boleyn, to be legitimate. Given their reputation, Henry was particularly concerned to seek the Carthusians' approval, and especially that of the prior of London who was also 'visitor' or inspector of all the English houses. When the commissioners arrived at the London charterhouse on 4 May, Prior Houghton and his community took the view that it was not their concern, being only Carthusian monks. Perhaps unwisely, they went on to say that they were not persuaded that the king's first marriage was not valid. Prior Houghton and his procurator Humphrey Middlemore were dispatched to the Tower forthwith. Their imprisonment was reasonably gentle and subtle pressure was applied, particularly by Edward Lee, the Archbishop of York. Houghton and Middlemore agreed to allow the community to take the oath and were released; after some prevarication, the House of the Salutation affirmed the oath on 6 June. The other houses took their lead from London, and it seemed for a short while that the crisis was past. There was only one exception; two monks of Mount Grace refused to swear, but this was quietly forgotten about and they were lodged in the priory prison.

In November 1534, the Act of Succession was followed by an Act of Supremacy, stating the king to be 'the only supreme head in earth of the church in England', and in February 1535 by the Treason Act which included treason by word and specifically such speech as might 'maliciously' deprive the king of any of his 'dignities or titles'. The Act of Supremacy did not require an oath, but this did not stop commissioners being appointed to administer one. Priors Houghton, Laurence, and Webster decided to forestall the commissioners by appealing directly to Thomas Cromwell, the king's secretary who was also his Vicar General in matters religious, asking to be exempted from the oath. This was rejected and the three were committed to the Tower. On their refusal to sign the oath they were sent for trial at Westminster Hall on 28 April 1535, charged with 'falsely, maliciously, and traitorously saying that the king our sovereign lord is not supreme head in earth of the church of England'. After a two-day trial, their conviction resulted more from Cromwell's threats than the jurors' opinion, and they were hanged, drawn and quartered in their habits at Tyburn. If the crown could not count on their support, it intended to make an example of them.

The execution of the three Carthusian priors did not end the matter. The London community would not accept the royal supremacy, even after the execution of the procurator and two others. Because of the community's reputation, Cromwell did not openly go any further. Instead, he intruded two of his servants into the house to oppress the remaining monks and to browbeat them individually. Four who refused to be coerced were packed off to Beauvale and Hull, the community was split, and all but ten of the monks accepted the oath. Those who still refused were dispatched to Newgate prison in May 1537 where they were left to starve to death.

At Mount Grace, second only in reputation to London, Prior Wilson was initially minded to refuse to accept the royal supremacy. He took council of Archbishop Lee and Bishop Tunstall of Durham, both conservative churchmen who had accepted the supremacy with different degrees of hesitation. On 9 July 1535 he had a private interview with the archbishop, who reported to Cromwell that he was now compliant. He had some difficulty with his community, however, for a monk and a lay brother refused to sign and fled to Scotland. They were brought back and placed in the priory prison until they complied. When Drs Layton and Legh visited Mount Grace late in the year to assess the quality of religious life, they found the community in agreement and the problems of July overcome.

At Witham, Hinton, Coventry, and Sheen, the communities had little problem in accepting either the royal supremacy or the king's divorce – or if they did knew better than to argue about it. The community at Axholme, bereft at the loss of their prior, began to break down and was unable to offer any resistance at all. At Beauvale, similarly deprived of its prior, Trafford the procurator affirmed his belief in papal supremacy and his willingness to die for it. Consequently he was dispatched to London for an interview with Cromwell. There, his determination deserted him and he was packed off to Sheen and later put in charge of the remnants of the London community. Otherwise, the brothers at Beauvale assented. At Hull, two members of the London house sent there when Cromwell tried to break the Carthusians' resolve stood firm, though the rest of the community accepted the royal supremacy. The London monks were removed to York, indicted for treason, and executed. Thus with the exception of London, the charterhouses acquiesced to the royal will, though not without a degree of unwillingness. They still retained their reputation for devotion. When royal commissioners visited Hull in 1535 to compile the *Valor Ecclesiasticus* (Worth of the Church) they were required to record the taxable income and allowable expenditure of the house, but additionally were to report on the standing of the community. They recorded that the monks were 'well-favoured and commended by the honest men of Hull for their good living and great hospitality'. Given the government's attempts to destroy the Carthusians' standing with the outside world this was not the comment that was expected and the King actually suggested that his commissioners had been bribed. The commissioners, however, stood their ground.

One of the purposes of the *Valor* (**80**) was to establish which monasteries were viable and which were not, for the King was about to begin a reform of the church which had been long overdue. There was a widespread belief in the early sixteenth century that many monks were no longer performing adequately the duties that the founders of the monasteries had required. In many houses, religious life was breaking

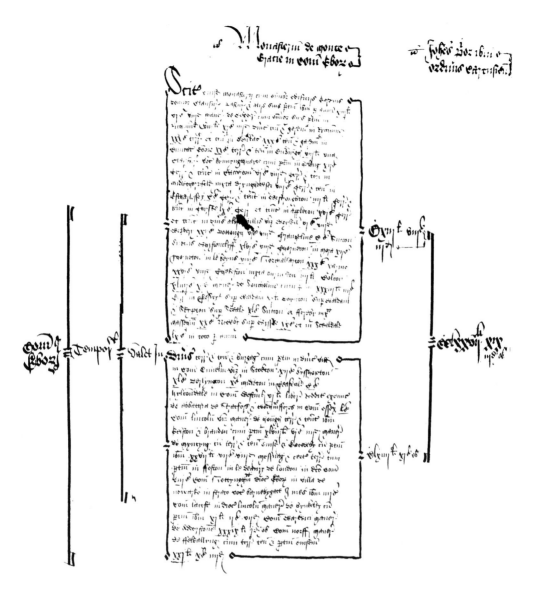

80 *The* Valor Ecclesiaticus *entry for Mount Grace (Public Record Office)*

down, and in a very small number even the regular singing of the offices was being ignored. The government chose in 1536 to place a bill before Parliament for the suppression of the smaller monasteries where 'manifest sin, vicious, carnal, and abominable living' was daily practiced. The inmates might be released from monastic life (but not their vows), or transfer to one of the 'divers and great solemn monasteries, wherein, thanks be to God, religion is right well kept and observed'. The definition of a great and solemn monastery was one with a net income of £200. The Act of Suppression of April 1536 caught four Carthusian monasteries, Beauvale,

133

Coventry, Axholme, and Hull and they would have been suppressed but for two reasons: no monks wished to leave their monastic seclusion, and none of the larger houses with the exception of London had any spaces. Given the problems that London continued to present, Cromwell was not going to put more monks in the empty cells there. Closing the poorer Carthusian houses was not an option for the time being, though Hull, Beauvale, and Coventry had to purchase their continuance.

The suppression of 1538-9

Two events which did not involve the Carthusians led directly to the suppression of all their houses in England; the Lincolnshire Rising and the great Yorkshire revolt, the Pilgrimage of Grace, both in 1536. Caused by the suppression of the lesser monasteries and a more general unhappiness with the government, the rebels coerced a number of monasteries to support them. Those abbots and priors who marched with the rebels, mainly because they had been threatened with the burning of their monasteries if they did not, were subsequently tried for treason and their houses seized by the Crown. The wealthy monasteries of Whalley, Bridlington, Jervaulx, and Barlings were taken, and the abbot of Furness, who was to a certain extent compromised, offered his monastery to the King before he was accused of treason. The government, faced with an expensive war with France, desperately needed money and what had begun as a reform of the monastic church changed to become a massive expropriation of church lands and buildings. Without the benefit of an act of Parliament, royal commissioners set out to persuade the religious to suppress themselves. The deposed presidents and monks would be given fairly generous pensions and found preferment in the church as soon as possible. The great houses began to fall, and the Carthusians were not immune, though to be fair to both the monks and the government, all but two held out until after Parliament had passed a retrospective Act for the dissolution of abbeys in 1539.

The suppression of Axholme 1538

After the death of their prior Augustine Webster, the Carthusians of Axholme were content to do whatever the government decreed and offered their procurator Thomas Barningham to Cromwell as a prior who would be compliant with the Crown. Barningham fell sick, and the vicar of the house, Michael Mekenes, described by Archishop Thomas Cranmer as of 'no learnyng, and 'very simple to be the governor of a house', stole the house's seal and set off for London where he was appointed prior unknown to his brothers. The disquiet this caused literally broke the community apart, and the monks had little option but to surrender their house to the King in June 1538.

There are indications that the government was interfering in the Carthusian community after the battle of wills lead by the London charterhouse in 1534-5 by imposing priors who would be compliant. The charterhouse of Sheen, adjacent to the royal palace of Richmond, had been shaken in the early 1530s when they had uncritically supported Elizabeth Barton, a visionary who had criticised the royal divorce, and as a result the community there had meekly assented to both the oaths of Succession and Supremacy without any fuss. The prior John Michell and procurator Henry Man were marked down by Cromwell as men likely to do his bidding. Man was subsequently appointed prior of Sheen (and thus visitor of the English province), and Michell was dispatched to Witham, both men working towards the government's requirements. The end of the remaining charterhouses was fast approaching, and Sheen itself began to be broken up in 1538, though it lingered on into the following year.

In the summer of 1538, the remaining monks of the London charterhouse had placed their monastery in the King's hands, though they were not expelled and allowed to continue their religious lives. On 15 November, three days after the commissioners for the suppression arrived in Smithfield, the community was finally turned out.

The suppressions of 1539

The first houses to fall in 1539 were Witham and Hinton. At Witham, John Michell's task of softening up the community for surrender was apparently an easy one, and the house was suppressed on 15 March 1539. The neighbouring house of Hinton had been approached by the suppression commissioners on 27 January, and the prior Edmund Horde had pointedly said that he would surrender the house if the King ordered it, but as the King had not he refused. Horde had a good reputation within the order and was one of the last scholarly priors. Rather than coerce him, the commissioners withdrew and did not return until 30 March. The community surrendered itself the following day.

Coventry, Hull, and Mount Grace were all suspected by the government of complicity in the revolts of 1536-7, though it was never established beyond doubt, and Prior Wilson's initial reluctance to accept the oath of Supremacy had not been forgotten. Coventry and Hull were only functioning under licences to continue and could have been suppressed at any time. Coventry, under its last prior John Brocheard, surrendered on 18 January; Sheen was finally closed down on 10 October; and Hull under its prior Ralph Malevery capitulated on 9 November, leaving Mount Grace as the last house of the order in England. The suppression commissioners, Drs Layton and Legh, took the suppression of Mount Grace on 18 December.

The treatment of the ex-monks

All of the Carthusian monks who were displaced in 1538-9 were well treated in comparison with monks of other houses, and many seem to have left with the contents of their cells, some even took books from the library, and at least one of the London monks was allowed to take the panelling of his cell. All were awarded pensions and many would find later preferment in the church. Some, however, were treated more fairly than others: the average pension for a choir monk was about £6 10s (£6.50) though the highest pensioned paid to the London monks was £5 – the government had not forgiven their earlier intransigence. As well as the pension, which was paid annually in two instalments, a gratuity was given to each monk to provide for his immediate needs, usually equal to a full year's pension or just slightly less.

Priors were generally well rewarded; Henry Man of Sheen was rewarded for his pro-government stance with a pension of £133 6s 8d (£133.33), Michael Mekenes of Axholme received only £20, while John Wilson of Mount Grace was rewarded with £60 and a house and chapel called The Mount, formerly a hermitage, which had belonged to his charterhouse. Generally speaking, the value of the prior's pension reflected the value of his monastery. Only at Coventry was there any attempt to defraud the Crown in the process of suppression. Prior Brocherd busied himself with dispersing the house's lands on long leases and buried much of the plate to keep it out of the commissioners' hands, only to be denounced by a citizen of Coventry who had not benefited from the prior's largesse. The plate was recovered and somehow Brocherd retained his pension.

The evidence from excavation at Coventry and Mount Grace is that the cells were stripped bare at the suppression, and it might be expected that the goods were sold at auction as at other houses. Dr London, the commissioner who suppressed Coventry, however, recorded that he had 'given each brother his whole cell saving the house and one vestment', and the will of William Bee, late monk of Mount Grace, who died in Newcastle in 1551, listed a set of household goods almost identical to those brought to Mount Grace from London by Thomas Golwynne in 1519. Almost certainly, each member of the community was allowed to take what he wanted from his own cell, more generous treatment than normally occurred, since the Crown was usually concerned to recover as much money as possible.

It would seem that some members of the various communities kept in contact after the suppression. William Bee of Mount Grace left two pairs of spectacles with silver frames to his ex-prior John Wilson, all save one of his books, his cloak, and his lantern to his ex-brother Leonard Hall, and one shilling each to all of his professed brothers from Mount Grace. When Queen Mary restored a community to Sheen in 1555, John Wilson and Leonard Hall, together with the lay brethren John Saunderson and Robert Shipley, were part of that short-lived house. It is quite likely that several members of each community managed to maintain their eremitic life outside the confines of their monasteries.

The conversion of the charterhouses to mansions

Many monasteries were converted into substantial houses after their suppression, for their layout around a cloister was not dissimilar to the great houses of the sixteenth century, and the only requirements of the leases on which the sites were granted out

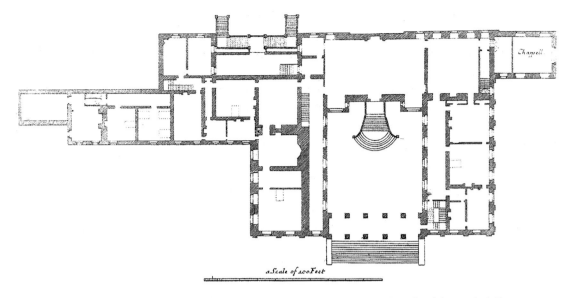

81 *Plan of the ground floor of the Wyndham mansion at Witham. The thick walls of the north (left) wing show that it was part of the Carthusian church From Colen Campbell's* Vitruvius Britannicus

was that the church and chapter house should be defaced. Defaced did not necessarily mean demolished. Every one of the Carthusian monasteries was converted in the sixteenth or seventeenth century into a house of some sort.

In 1544, Witham was granted to Sir Ralph Hopton who appears to have created a house on the site, though its form is unknown. Certainly he was buried at Witham in 1571. The site passed to his great nephew, Sir Robert Hopton, and both he and his son Sir Ralph were resident at Witham. The house was besieged three times during the Civil War campaigns in the south-west, and was 'strengthened' in 1644. While survey (**10**) identified no evidence for this post-suppression house or Civil War activity, it did identify a potentially mid-seventeenth-century layout surviving in the gardens of its known early eighteenth-century successor.

The Witham site passed by marriage to John Wyndham in the late seventeenth century, and remained in the family's possession until it was sold to Sir William Beckford of Fontill before 1763. It was Sir William Wyndham who commissioned William Talman to 'improve' his residence in 1717, work which was completed by James Gibbs. A plan of the *piano nobile* and elevation of this building is known (**81**), indicating the addition of a southern wing and western enclosing portico or screen to an existing house. The earthworks of this are still visible in the north-eastern part of the site, immediately to the south of the railway, the plan of the building being substantially confirmed by geophysics. The steps up to the portico on its west side survive as a rectangular mound. The north wing of the house was apparently converted from the monastic church.

The formal garden relates closely to the house as it was in 1717. However, it is clear from the design that it is a mid-seventeenth-century creation. The earthworks articulate well on plan with the building, although when seen on the ground they are not coherent because of their differing states of preservation. The approach to the house was from the west where there was a rectangular walled court measuring 58 x 40m and defined by strong scarps to north and south, cut through obliquely by the railway. Its western side is obscured by hedges, the railway, and landfill in the field to the west, though it is clear that the western side of the court was polygonal, perhaps a half-octagon. The approach to the house would have arrived here from the north-west, close to the present bridge over the Frome. A broad bank with flanking ditches connects the west end of the court with the road to the bridge and is undoubtedly the drive. On its western side and square to the axis of the entrance court is a substantial platform with traces of buildings in the form of rectangular hollows and scarps, perhaps a lodge or later agricultural buildings. The main garden lay to the south of the house and corresponds with the area of the great cloister of the charterhouse. There was no access from the principal suite of rooms in the south wing of the house, but there was from an elaborate flight of steps on the eastern side that led to a long north-south walk which ran along the east side of the house and continued southwards along the eastern side of the former great cloister. Below it is a level area or terrace where slight scarps indicate former garden features. The great cloister was retained as a privy or walled garden, and the tiled alleys appear to have been maintained, for excavation produced a coin of 1672 associated with it. A survey of 1761 records 'the lead on the ridge and on the Cornish over the Terras Walk' and 'on the Terras Walk' suggesting that either the east cloister alley or its extension to the north was roofed. Geophysical survey has confirmed that the cloister garth contained a symmetrical arrangement of garden beds. The extent of the south garden was defined by a massive terrace with an external ditch on the south and western sides, though the ditch on the west side has been filled. On the east, the field boundary itself marks a change in level of 1.3m, representing the continuation of the main terrace along the eastern side of both house and garden. This terrace overlooked the ponds in the valley below. At the south-west corner of the privy garden, on a corner of the main terrace, is a sub-rectangular mound 0.6m high, which was the site of a summerhouse or pavilion at the highest point of the garden. The stables and service ranges lay to the north of the house and now lie below the railway. To their west was the 'great garden' that extended the length of the forecourt. Its northern extent is obscured by the modern road and the buildings of Witham Hall Farm.

This was not the final development at Witham, for Sir William Beckford began a new house in 1762, some 250m to the south of the Wyndham house to a design by Robert Adam (**82**). Its plan and elevation were recorded by Colen Campbell in 1771, and its site was located by survey (**10**). Demolished by William Beckford who was concentrating on the construction of Fonthill Abbey between 1770-88, the house had a central block of two storeys above a basement with a full height portico connected by open colonnades to flanking pavilions. The central block, symmetrical wings, and eastern pavilion can be clearly identified. Some internal divisions are visible, as well as robbed walling. On the south front two rectangular

82 *William Beckford's mansion at Witham designed by Robert Adam. From Colen Campbell's* Vitruvius Britannicus

hollows mark the site of the staircases that led to the main entrance. The mansion was built on the summit of a gentle rounded hill, an elevation which was emphasized by raising terraces against its north and south facades, facing south-east into Witham Park. A new access drive was built on this side of the house, some 2.8km long. It still survives over most of its length as a cambered track with flanking ditches or as a double hedgerow, and for 2km it is aligned on the earlier house, suggesting that part of it was intended to be retained as an 'eye-catcher'. It then turned to the north-west and began to climb the knoll on which the new house stood, its line still marked by a double hedgerow with a cambered drive flanked by ditches. To the south of the house, a low curving scarp marks a circular carriage sweep at the end of the drive. No landscaping associated with this house has been identified and almost certainly none was undertaken, as the house was demolished before it was completed. However, the building of two great mansions on the site and one more to the south-west would suggest that most of the earthwork remains at Witham are not those of the charterhouse.

Hinton was granted to Sir Walter Hungerford immediately after its suppression, but before he could do anything with the site Sir Thomas Arundel, who had been sent to survey the site, demolished and carried away the greater part of the church. Before his complaint to Cromwell could be investigated, Hungerford had been disgraced and executed and Hinton was back in royal hands. The site was sold to John and Robert Bartlett, speculators in monastic property, in 1546. They sold the site on to Mathew Colthurst, whose son sold it back to the Hungerfords in 1578. When John Leland saw the site in the early 1540s, many of the buildings had already gone and all he recorded in his *Itinerary* was 'a graung (barn) great and well builded'. While the church had been dismantled it is clear that the chapter house and prior's cell and refectory had been retained, together with the enclosure of the great cloister, intending that this should form the basis of a new house. Because there was no need of a house until 1578, this idea was not taken up, and when the Hungerfords built their new house in the 1580s it was on the north side of the precinct, partly re-using the precinct wall and a medieval building placed against it (**83**). Post-suppression modification of the charterhouse earthworks is limited to the area around the sixteenth-century house and its steading. To the south of the manor house is a broad

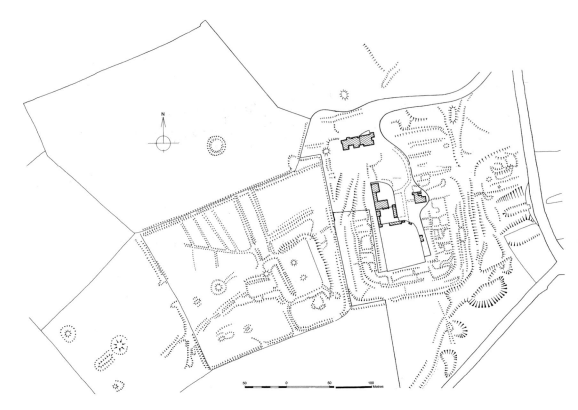

83 *The site at Hinton today, with the manor house placed against the northern precinct wall*

linear hollow some 10m wide with a bank 8m wide and 0.3m high on its east side, and tree mounds have been created on the western side of the precinct boundary and within the fields to the west. The great cloister was retained as a farm yard, with some cells being modified to serve as animal houses, their cloister doors blocked and back walls removed. Parts of the north range of the cloister were retained but the church and buildings of the inner court were demolished. By the late eighteenth century the cloister garth had become an orchard, and by 1849 was the 'new garden'.

Beauvale was granted to Sir John Hussey, who like Sir Walter Hungerford had fallen foul of the government and been executed in 1539. Possession was confirmed to his son, Sir William, in 1541. Significantly, it is the land that is referred to and not simply the buildings of the charterhouse, and because Sir William Hussey put the charterhouse in dower for his wife and children, it would appear that there was never any intention of building a grand house. The church and part of the north side of the great cloister was retained, presumably to form the nucleus of a house, but no substantial rebuilding took place until the last decades of the sixteenth century, when the retained part of the north cloister range was raised in height. By the early eighteenth century this house was in ruins, and the site was occupied by the farmhouse which still exists (**84**). Because the earthworks are so clear and relate closely to the known plan of the medieval buildings, it is unlikely that the house ever developed a formal garden.

84 *The ruins of the church at Beauvale and the eighteenth-century farmhouse that lies on top of the east cloister range*

The London charterhouse was initially held by the king, and the church was used for the storage of the king's tents and garden equipment. It was converted to a mansion by Lord North and the Duke of Norfolk from the middle years of the sixteenth century, and this still stands on the north-western post-Roman boundary of the city. Although the church was demolished, a courtyard house was built around the lesser cloister, and the chapter house was retained as the chapel of the new house. The doors of the cells in the great cloister were blocked up, and that area became an enclosed garden that survived until the late 1950s.

The charterhouse of Coventry was retained by the Court of Augmentations, the body set up to administer the estates of suppressed monasteries, and it seems to have survived undamaged until it was sold to two speculators, Richard Andrews and

Leonard Chamberlain, in 1542. Lead from the roofs which was reserved to the King was being cast down in 1543, and the fact that 55 tons of this were recovered suggests that the principal buildings had lead roofs, unusual in a Carthusian context. The prior's cell and refectory seem to have been retained with the intention of converting them into a house. The site passed through a number of hands before it was acquired by Sampson Baker before 1584. It was Baker who converted the surviving buildings into a fairly small house, for his name appears in an inscription on one of the inserted first floor walls in the old refectory. The building was re-windowed in the late eighteenth century, but today survives largely in the state that Sampson Baker remodeled it (**colour plate 23**).

Axholme charterhouse was sold to John Candysshe of West Butterwick in 1540 for £348 8s 4d (£348.42), and he must have begun remodeling and building immediately, because John Leland who saw the site in the early 1540s observed

> by Milwood park stoode the right fair monasterie of the carthusianes, wher one of the Mulbrais dukes of Northfolk was buried in a tumbe of alabaster. Mr Candisch hath now turned the monastery to a goodly manor place.

The post-suppression house occupied the north side of a cloister and was defined by a wet moat on the west (now backfilled), south and east sides (**16**). This mansion was described by Abraham de la Pryme, a north Lincolnshire clergyman, in 1698 from his recollection of the building as a youth:

> I can remember very well that [it] was a great and most stately building of many stories high, all of huge squared stone, all wholly built so upon vaults and arches that I have gone under the same a great way. All was huge stone staircases, huge pillars, long entries, with the doors of both sides opening into opposite rooms. I remember the dining room also, which was at the end of one of those entries, had huge long tables in it, great church windows, with a great deal of painted glass. The outside of the house was all beautified with semi-arches jutting off the walls upon channeled pillars, and the top was all covered in lead. The doors were huge and strong, and ascended unto by a great many steps, and places made through the opposite turrets to defend the same, and the whole was encompassed with a huge ditch or moat . . . there was also the finest gardens, orchards and flowers there that I ever saw; but now there is, I believe, none of these things to be seen, for about 10 years ago, all or most part being ruinous was pulled down and a lesser house built out of the same.

This second house remains in part within a surviving farmhouse and one of its outbuildings.

The site of the post-suppression house appears to have occupied the whole of the north range of the great cloister, and it may have incorporated the priory church. A medieval pier surviving in the basement of the later house may still be in its original

85 *Thomas Lascelles' manor house at Mount Grace before it was extended in 1900*

position. To the south, the area of the cloister has been modified by the creation of a formal garden, features associated with which extend well beyond the moated area.

Mount Grace was leased to a speculator, John Cheney of Drayton in Buckinghamshire for a period of 21 years in February 1540, though the next year, probably following the intial stripping of the site, the lease was surrendered and acquired by a local landowner, Sir James Strangways of East Harsley. Strangways lived in East Harlsey castle and had no need of a new house; it was the land that went with the charterhouse that he wanted. There might also have been a desire to protect his parents' tombs in the church. Parts of the site, particularly the prior's cell and refectory and the kitchen, had been taken down in 1539, possibly with the conversion of the site to a mansion intended, but this work had been discontinued and there was no further destruction. The guest house range seems to have retained its roof, because three of the trusses in the present version contain elements of medieval base crucks, but there is no evidence to show that the building was altered to serve a new use in the sixteenth century. It may have been that some of the buildings of the inner court were simply retained as farm buildings.

The site was bought in 1653 by Thomas Lascelles for £1900, and he converted the southern half of the guest house range to a modest manor house in the following year (**85**). His initials and the date 1654 are carved into the head of the door in the

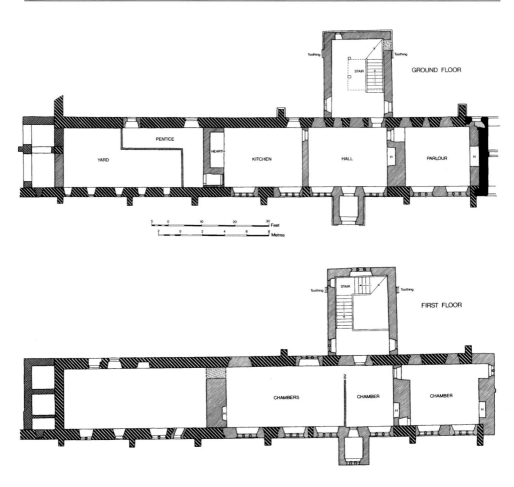

86 *The ground and first floor plans of Thomas Lascelles' house of 1654*

tower porch that he built. In plan (**86**), the building is very conservative; a central hall on the ground floor with a parlour to the south and a kitchen to the north, bedrooms on the first floor, and garrets in the roof. Access to the upper floors required a new wing on the back of the house that contains the stair, and it was intended that rooms would be built to either side of this flight. Toothings were provided to tie in new walls, but they were never built, probably because Lascelles had run out of money. The great cloister was turned into a walled garden as at Witham and London, and several of the cells on the north and west sides of the cloister retained their seventeenth-century blockings until the late nineteenth century. A garden was laid out on the site of the first prior's cell, and the south range of the inner court seems to have been retained as stables and granaries for the house. Quite remarkably, there does not seem to have been a serious attempt to clear away any of the monastic ruins apart from sporadic stone-robbing. The seventeenth-century house was almost doubled in size in 1900-01, when the ruins were laid out for display.

Sheen had a valuable riverside site adjacent to the royal palace of Richmond. In 1542, Henry VIII granted the site to Edward Seymour, brother of his third wife, Jane Seymour, lord high admiral and lord great chamberlain. Seymour began the conversion of the buildings to a suitable house. For the man who was to become Protector during the minority of the young Edward VI in 1547, it can be assumed that his house was a grand one, for Seymour was a noted builder. His fall, however, was as rapid as his rise, for in 1550 he was deprived of the protectorate, and he was executed as a felon two years later. The house at Sheen, along with his other estates, were seized by the Crown and given to Henry Grey, Duke of Suffolk, the father of Lady Jane Grey. Ownership of Sheen seems to have been fairly unlucky, for Suffolk rebelled against Mary I's marriage to Philip II of Spain and was executed for treason in 1554. Queen Mary granted the house to Anne Stanhope, Edward Seymour's widow. Because of Suffolk's short tenure and Anne Stanhope's loan of the house it is quite probable that nothing was done to Seymour's house until it was given back to the Carthusians in November 1555. Buildings were demolished, others were rebuilt, and the house of Jesus of Bethlehem was re-established, only to be suppressed again by Elizabeth in July 1559. The site was to remain in royal hands until the death of Charles I, though it was regularly leased out. A survey undertaken for Parliament in 1649 identifies a series of lodgings rather than a single house, each made up of an element of the monastery, the largest of which was still called the prior's lodging and the smallest 'anchorites' cells'.

The study of Carthusian monasteries

The study of the Carthusians only began seriously in 1896 when the Yorkshire Archaeological Society invited Sir William St John Hope, Assistant Secretary of the Society of Antiquaries of London and the leading authority on medieval monasteries, to excavate at Mount Grace Priory. Hope was slowly undertaking a monumental comparative study of monasteries of different orders, and in the course of his career he surveyed and excavated four Benedictine, two Cluniac, six Cistercian, four Augustinian, six Premonstratensian, one Templar, and two Carthusian houses, as well as one Augustinian nunnery and two houses of friars. He defined for the first time a 'typical' Carthusian plan at Mount Grace, and transcribed the vast archive of documents that described the London charterhouse. His research enthused others, and his rapid publication of Mount Grace made his ideas easily available. He was often wrong in his detailed conclusions but this was not important. He got the general picture right and he published his findings, allowing subsequent generations to build on his work.

It was Hope's work at Mount Grace that led directly to the Thoroton Society of Nottinghamshire's work at Beauvale in 1908. While Mount Grace had spectacular standing ruins, Beauvale was poorly preserved and largely below ground. It was by studying Hope's plan of Mount Grace that the Rev du Boulay Hill and Harry Gill were able to identify buried buildings from their earthworks, and to reconstruct a plan from a limited number of trenches. Both sites had, in fact, been studied with a remarkable economy of excavation, leaving them more or less intact for future excavation.

Nothing further happened until after the First World War. In 1918, attention turned to Witham where the site of the upper house had been relocated from the study of documents, an identification confirmed by small-scale trenching. Perhaps it is the sheer scale of Carthusian monasteries, coupled with the poor survival of standing fabric, that is off-putting, because this work was not followed up. Attention appears to have been taken by the work which was being undertaken on the great northern monastic sites by the Office of Works under Sir Charles Peers, and in the 1920s and 30s no serious work was undertaken on any Carthusian sites.

Bomb damage to the London charterhouse and its subsequent repair and reconstruction provided an opportunity for W.F. Grimes to test Hope's reconstruction of the church and lesser cloister, which had been based only on a study of the documents and the surviving buildings (**87**). Again this work was published quickly, and served as a catalyst for further work. Grimes was able to demonstrate both that Hope had in fact been wrong, and that there was plenty of scope for a renewed study of the Carthusians.

The surviving buildings at Hinton had been inspected by Office of Works architects in the late 1930s but they were unable to say where the great cloister lay, surprisingly because its earthworks were clearly visible. However, in 1950 the owner, Major Philip Fletcher, decided that he wanted to know more about the site and began a series of excavations that gradually revealed the plan, and in the early 1950s Dr Ralegh Radford undertook the first detailed examination of the surviving buildings. Though both studies were imperfect they stimulated interest in the site and encouraged further work at Witham in 1960. The problem in both cases was the small scale of the work and the resulting inability to distinguish medieval from post-medieval buildings. Nevertheless, this work provides the only information we currently have on these sites.

If the modern study of the Carthusians had begun at Mount Grace it was also rejuvenated by the site being taken into the care of the state and opened to the public on the death of its owner Sir Maurice Bell in 1953. Remarkably, the decision was taken not to excavate the site, but to strip it of fallen rubble and hill-wash under the most casual of archaeological supervision. It was assumed that Hope had done enough work to make the ruins intelligible, and all the efforts of the Ministry of Works were concentrated on conserving the standing ruins, a major undertaking in itself. It was only when clearance indicated that the site was more complicated than it was originally thought that Andrew Saunders was asked to excavate part of a single cell in 1957, and Martin Biddle to oversee early work on the well houses that Hope had not found. It is probable that very little damage was actually done to medieval deposits in the church and cells of the east range of the great cloister and lesser cloister when post-suppression deposits were stripped away, but considerable damage was done when a sewer was laid across the kitchen with no archaeological supervision at all. Post-suppression deposits which would have explained the process of ruination were removed in large areas without record, but a detailed plan was recovered that enabled the site to be laid out in exemplary fashion.

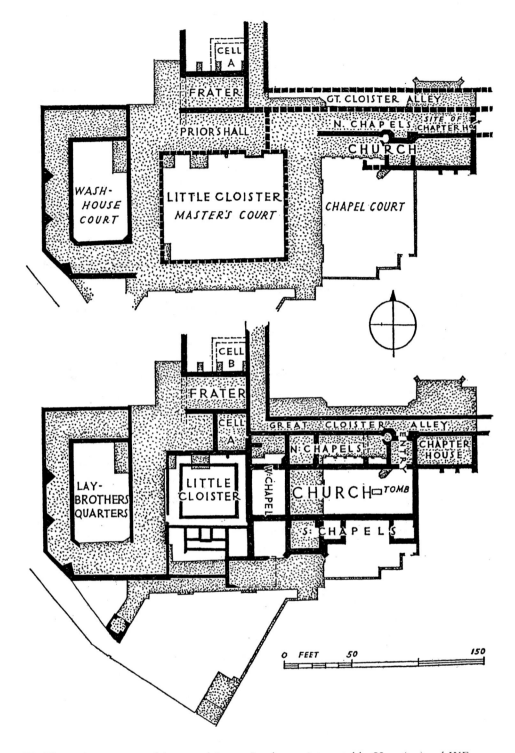

87 *The south-west corner of the great cloister at London, as interpreted by Hope (top) and W.F. Grimes (below)*

Hope had not excavated the west range of the great cloister because it was covered with trees, and when its display was proposed the decision was taken to carry out a proper excavation. Laurence Keen began work in 1967 and continued until 1971, returning for a final season in 1974 when his work was extended into the north range. For the first time anywhere, Carthusian cells and gardens had been excavated to a modern standard and substantial cultural collections recovered. Quite remarkably, modern standards of archaeology came late to monastic studies, and Keen's work at Mount Grace was one of the first excavations to show the potential for the re-excavation of sites which had been examined in the nineteenth century. Although his work was completed in 1974, Keen had only examined a small part of the site, and attention moved from Carthusian archaeology to a study of the Cistercians which began in the mid 1970s, driven by research excavations at Bordesley and Fountains and continued into the late 1980s. In many ways, the study of Cistercian monasteries was simpler, the priorities for research had been established for some time, and the international character of the Cistercian order encouraged research throughout Europe. Of course, the Carthusian order was equally international, but nowhere was anyone working on its archaeology.

Glyn Coppack was invited to excavate a single cell to complete the study of Mount Grace in 1985 when English Heritage took the bold decision to reconstruct Cell 8 on the north side of the great cloister, a building which had originally been rebuilt before 1905. The interest this caused led directly to the proposal to excavate the water tower, prior's cell, refectory, and kitchen from 1987, a project which was conceived as a piece of research to answer specific questions about the origins and development of the charterhouse, and to examine for the first time the common buildings of a Carthusian monastery. The completion of this work in 1992 revealed for the first time the sequence of building and enabled the growth of the monastery to be seen in the context of late medieval monastic life in general.

Almost in parallel with the work at Mount Grace was the excavation of the church and four cells of the Coventry charterhouse by Coventry Museums between 1968-87 under the direction of Brian Hobley, Margaret Rylatt, and Iain Soden. The two sites together provide the best evidence for the development of Carthusian charterhouses in England.

Future research

There remain, however, substantial areas of ignorance that need to be addressed before our knowledge of the Carthusians can approach that of the other regular orders. The monks of the order remain, for the most part, anonymous, and no Carthusian cemetery has ever been excavated (apart from the site of five graves in the cloister of the London charterhouse and two in the south cloister alley at Mount Grace). Little is known about the age or health of the communities, though documentary evidence would suggest that longevity was more common in a charterhouse than in contemporary Benedictine houses, where life expectancy was falling in the fifteenth and early sixteenth centuries. Their burials are likely to remain undisturbed within the identifiable cloister gardens of all the English houses, uncontaminated by patronal burials and easily accessible for excavation.

The development of the Carthusian cell and its garden remains substantially unstudied, thought it is central to the understanding of how the order evolved. In contrast, the process of development is well understood in other reformed orders and among the friars. Although the Carthusian order proudly maintains it is *nunquam reformata quia nunquam deformata* (never reformed because never deformed), it is clear that there is a development, but the process has not been examined by excavation. At Witham there is likely to be the full progression from documented timber cells to the 'late' cell-type identified by excavation, the cells at Hinton probably demonstrate development throughout the thirteenth century and there remains the possibility that the known cell plan at Beauvale represents a rebuilding to match the 'late' design first seen at London. There is also a variation in the planning of cells within individual contemporary houses that needs to be addressed. Similarly, the development of the lay brethren' accommodation from correrie through communal quarters (as suggested at London) to individual cells remains unexplored. Indeed, there has been no modern excavation of any lay brethren' accommodation on any site, partly because the lay brethren have been seen as a less important manifestation of Carthusian life, though that indicates a failure to understand the organisation of Carthusian communities.

The development of water systems remains unclear. While London, Beauvale, Mount Grace and most probably Sheen have a centralised water-tower, it would appear that Witham, Hinton, and possibly Axholme do not. A water supply was established in the early years of the Grande Chartreuse, and the technology was generally available from well before the foundation of Witham. At Hinton, the supply and drainage appear to have been confused by the excavators, while at Witham neither system has been identified. Different houses appear to have had widely differing methods of dealing with human excrement, yet monks moved between the houses of the order in England and must have been aware of the variations of provision they found. The Carthusians were a highly centralised order like the Cistercians, yet there does not appear to be a common approach to something as basic as water management. This can either be a result of differing levels of development, or the simple fact that it was not important within the order. Given the care which was evident in the engineering of supply and waste provision at Mount Grace, the latter seem unlikely.

The place of the Carthusians in the late medieval monastic church has yet to be established, partly because too much emphasis has been placed on the development of other orders in the twelfth and thirteenth centuries. Historically, a great deal is known but this has not been matched by archaeological research. It is clear that there was a renaissance in monastic life generally from the late fourteenth century, and there is evidence that the communal orders were beginning to favour individual cells on the Carthusian or collegiate model. The Carthusians were attracting both Augustinian and Premonstratensian canons to their cloisters, yet it is uncertain how far the Carthusian ideal had already spread outside their houses. Mount Grace has established that monks of the order enjoyed as good a lifestyle as other monks, and that the use of imported pottery was consistent with its use by other orders. Generally, there was a movement away from the strictness of the early twelfth-century Customs, but this was common to other orders as well. The Carthusians remained at heart 'Christ's Poor Men', although the framework of their religious lives reflected their high social status. The obvious link with the friars and particularly the Franciscans remains to be made.

Although considerable energy has been expended on understanding how other orders created and managed their estates, this has not been done for the Carthusians in spite of the fact that they were doing it at a time for which the surviving documentary evidence is good. That they were doing it in a different way to the Benedictines and Cistercians is apparent from the dispersed nature of their holdings, reflecting their endowment with alien priory estates. Precisely how they were accomplishing this remains a mystery, yet half the houses of the order in England enjoyed a high level of income which is apparent in their buildings and material culture.

Further reading

Information on the Carthusians is very difficult to find in print and much of what is published is now seriously out of date, and so needs to be read with caution.

Two recent publications by Mick Aston set the scene: 'The development of the Carthusian order in Europe and Britain: a preliminary survey' in M. Carver (ed) *In Search of Cult: Archaeological Investigations in Honour of Philip Rahtz* (Boydell, Woodbridge, 1993), and 'The Expansion of the Monastic and Religious Orders of Europe from the Eleventh Century' in G. Keevil, M. Aston & T. Hall (eds) *Monastic Archaeology: Papers on the Study of Medieval Monasteries* (Oxbow, Oxford, 2001). For St Bruno, his entry in David Hugh Farmer's *Oxford Dictionary of Saints* (Oxford University Press, Oxford, 1992) is by far the best starting point, followed by the Benedictine Monks of St Augustine's Abbey Ramsgate's *The Book of Saints* (Cassell, London, 1989). The early years of the order are described in J-P. Aniel's *Les Maisons des Chartreux: des origins à la Chartreuse de Pavie* (Bibliotheque de la Société Francaise d'Archéologie, Droz, Geneva, 1983) and *La Grande Chartreuse* par un Chartreux (14th edn, La Sadag, Ain, France, 1984). For an English source see E. Margaret Thompson's *The Carthusian Order in England* (SPCK, London, 1930).

For Carthusian planning and buildings, there are a number of sources. The most accessible is Wolfgang Braunfels' *Monasteries of Western Europe: The Architecture of the Orders* (Thames and Hudson, London, 1972) where a whole chapter is devoted to the order. Much more instructive are the four volumes of *Maisons de l'Ordre des Chartreux* published between 1913-19 by the charterhouses of Notre Dame des Prés and Parkminster in Sussex. Views of almost all surviving charterhouses and the standing ruins in England make up these volumes, and they provide remarkable insight into the scale and planning of the monasteries.

For the history of the English houses of the order, see Margaret Thompson's *The Carthusian Order in England* and her earlier *A History of the Somerset Carthusians* (SPCK, London, 1900). Though Miss Thompson's work is sound it is now very dated and a considerable amount of documentary work has been done since she first published. Used with care however, these books provide an excellent introduction to the English houses. The archaeological study of the Carthusians in England began with Sir William St John Hope's excavation at Mount Grace and his long-term study of the London charterhouse. His 'Architectural Description of Mount Grace Charterhouse' is published in Volume 18 of the *Yorkshire Archaeological Journal* (1905), and his London research *The History of the London Charterhouse from its Foundation until the Suppression* (SPCK, London, 1925) was completed and published posthumously. Almost as important was the post-war excavation of the London

Charterhouse by W.F. Grimes, which recovered the plan of the church and corrected Hope's interpretation. His work is fully described in David Knowles and W. F. Grimes *Charterhouse: The Medieval Foundation in the light of recent discoveries* (Longman, Green and Co., London, 1954). Hope's work at Mount Grace, undertaken when monastic archaeology was still in its infancy, has also been overtaken by more recent work. A review of his interpretation is included in Glyn Coppack and Laurence Keen's forthcoming *Mount Grace Priory: The Excavations of 1957-92* (English Heritage monograph).

For individual sites, the material available in print is limited. The small scale excavations at Witham are published in Ian and Cathy Burrow's 'Witham Priory: The First English Carthusian Monastery', in *Proceedings of the Somerset Archaeological and Natural History Society*, 134 (1990). Work at Hinton in the 1950s appears in two articles by P. C. Fletcher: 'Recent Excavations at Hinton Priory' in *Proceedings of the Somerset Archaeological and Natural History Society*, 96 (1951) and 'Further Excavations at Hinton Priory' in *Proceedings of the Somerset Archaeological and Natural History Society*, 103 (1958-9). These are usefully reviewed with additional material in James Hogg 'The Architecture of Hinton Charterhouse' in *Analecta Cartusiana*, 25 (1975). Extensive work at Beauvale in the early twentieth century is described in A. du Boulay Hill and H. Gill's 'Beauvale Charterhouse, Notts' in *Transactions of the Thoroton Society of Nottinghamshire*, 12 (1908). The recent excavations at Coventry are fully reported in Iain Soden's *Excavations at St Anne's Charterhouse, Coventry, 1968-87* (Coventry Museums Service, Coventry, 1995). Mount Grace is summarised in the site guide, Glyn Coppack's *Mount Grace Priory, North Yorkshire* (English Heritage, London, 1991). For Sheen see J Cloake 'Richmond's Great Monastery – the Charterhouse of Jesus of Bethlehem at Shene' in *Richmond Local History Society*, 6 (1990).

The Carthusians' use of water was first examined by Sir William St John Hope in his paper 'The London Charterhouse and its Old Water Supply' in *Archaeologia*, 58.1 (1903). More recently, this work has been re-examined by Glyn Coppack in two papers: 'La chartreuse de Mount Grace, le système hydraulique du 15e siècle: l'adduction, la distribution, et l'évacuation des eaux' in Leon Pressouyre (ed) *L'hydaulique monastique* (Créaphis, Grâne, France, 1996), and 'The contribution of the Carthusians to monastic hydraulics: the evidence from England' in Jose Mascarenhas, Maria Abecasis, and Virgilino Jorge (eds) *Hidraulica Monastica Medieval e Moderna* (Fundação Oriente, Lisbon, 1996). Related to this is a fascinating discussion of the health of English Carthusian monks by Dr Joseph Gribbin, 'Health and Disease in the English Charterhouses: a Preliminary Study' in *Analecta Cartusiana*, 157 (2001).

Gazetteer

Of the nine successful charterhouses in England, seven have substantial remains, either of standing buildings or earthworks. Only Mount Grace is regularly open to the public, but others can be visited by arrangement. Three are on pasture farmland, two are urban, and one lies within the gardens and paddocks of a private house. Only Hull and Sheen have left no visible traces.

Witham

The site of the charterhouse is marked by extensive earthworks to the south of Witham Hall Farm at National Grid Reference ST 758417 to the south-east of the village of Witham Friary where the correrie was located, 4 miles south of Frome in Somerset.

The earthworks, which are bisected by the Great Western railway line, mark not only the site of the monastery but a succession of post-medieval houses and their gardens. There has been limited excavation. A small collection of worked stone from the site, predominantly window tracery and columns, can be seen in the gardens of Witham Hall Farm and Witham Hole Cottage; further fragments survive in the churchyard of Witham Friary and built into cottages opposite the church. This material presumably derives from the correrie.

Hinton

The surviving buildings at Hinton are incorporated into the steading of a sixteenth century mansion, Hinton Abbey; the inner court buildings lie below its lawns, and the earthworks of the great cloister within an orchard and paddocks to the south of the house and its garden. The site is centred on National Grid Reference ST 777591 on the west side of the A36 4 miles south of Bath and 1 mile north-east of the village of Hinton Charterhouse in Somerset. There is no public access. The modern hamlet of Friary, to the east, marks the site of the correrie.

Surviving are the chapter house building and the prior's cell and refectory, both re-roofed and converted to agricultural use in the post-suppression period. Medieval masonry is also present in the late sixteenth-century house, the back wall of which retains a section of the precinct wall. The greater part of the layout of the site has been recovered by small-scale excavation, and the great cloister is marked by good quality earthworks. A collection of architectural detail recovered by excavation is stored in the prior's cell.

Beauvale

The site of the charterhouse is marked by the buildings of Beauvale Priory Farm, some 2 miles north east of Eastwood and 8 miles north-west of Nottingham at National Grid reference SK 492490 on the west side of the M1 Motorway between Junctions 26 and 27. There are both standing ruins and excellent earthworks.

The standing ruins comprise the church, now in a very dangerous and unrepaired state, a building at its south-west corner which was clearly part of a post-suppression conversion to a house, and the gatehouse. The earthworks, which are on pasture land, are remarkably clear and show the full extent of the site. There was limited excavation in 1908, and loose architectural detail can still be seen both in the garden of Beavale Priory Farm, and reused in the post-medieval farm buildings. Floor tiles from the site are in Nottingham Castle Museum and Nottingham University Museum.

London

The London charterhouse lies north of Charterhouse Square, to the north of Barbican tube station. The gatehouse and a part of the precinct wall are on the north side of the square. The post-suppression house which contains parts of the church, chapter house, lesser cloister, and cloister is occupied by Sutton's Hospital, the charity which is the basis of Charterhouse School. To the north is an open square on the site of the great cloister, enclosed by the buildings of London University Medical and Dental School (St Barts).

Coventry

The Coventry charterhouse lies on the north side of London Road, 2 miles from the centre of Coventry at National Grid Reference SP 344782. Today it is part of Tile Hill College and can be visited by arrangement.

Surviving are the prior's house and refectory, converted in the later sixteenth century to a house, the south wall of the church, and the greater part of the precinct wall. Within the garden, some of the cells on the east side of the great cloister have been laid out for display. The northern part of the precinct retains earthworks, now rather eroded, which mark the site of the outer and inner courts. There were substantial excavations in the 1960s and 70s which have recovered the plan of the church and eastern range of the great cloister. Finds from the site are in Coventry City Museum.

Hull

The Hull charterhouse lay on the north side of the medieval town at National Grid Reference TA 099293. There are no known remains and evaluation excavation failed to find the site, which is deeply buried by post-medieval deposits.

Axholme

The charterhouse of Axholme is marked by the modern Low Melwood Farm on the east side of the road between Epworth and Owston Ferry, 2 miles south-east of Epworth and 10 miles south-west of Scunthorpe in the Isle of Axholme in North Lincolnshire, centred on National Grid Reference SE 806019. The greater proportion of the site comprises pasture land, but some parts lie below modern farm buildings.

Axholme charterhouse was converted into a major house after the suppression, and it is now difficult to separate those earthworks which are monastic from the evidence of the later house and its garden. Small-scale excavation in 1968 has shown that monastic deposits survive well and that the buildings were of brick with stone dressings. One monastic building, part of the north range of the great cloister, survives within the present farm house, and parts of the later house remain in other farm buildings. To the west of the farmhouse, which is now derelict, is a pile of medieval and later architectural detail recovered from the site.

Mount Grace

The surviving ruins of Mount Grace Priory lie on the east side of the A19, 6 miles north-east of Northallerton and 16 miles south of Middlesborough in North Yorkshire, centred on National Grid Reference SE 449985. The site is owned by the National Trust and managed by English Heritage, and is the only site regularly open to the public.

The ruins of Mount Grace comprise the best preserved of the English charterhouses, with substantial remains of the church, great cloister, inner court, and the earthworks of the outer court with its fishponds. The guest house range was converted to a house in 1654 and now contains an introductory exhibition. The site was extensively excavated in 1896-1900, and again from 1957. Finds from the site are displayed in the guest house and are curated in the English Heritage archaeology store at Helmsley. There is a substantial collection of detached architectural fragments displayed on site and stored there.

Sheen

The royal charterhouse of Sheen at Richmond upon Thames now lies below the Royal Mid-Surrey Golf Club, immediately to the south of the Royal Botanic Gardens, Kew, at National Grid Reference TQ 170756. There are no visible remains.

Glossary

Apse	The rounded eastern termination of a church, chapel, or similar building, regularly used in other European countries by the Carthusians but not used in England.
Bay	The structural division of a building, normally emphasised in its architecture by vertical divisions such as buttresses, and in its roof by tie-beams.
Cell	The enclosed house and garden, and its contents, occupied by a Carthusian monk. Normally, it only applies to a partitioned space in the communal buildings of other orders.
Chapter house	The room where the community met to discuss business, confess faults, and receive penance. In Carthusian monasteries it contained an altar.
Charterhouse	The English name given to Carthusian monasteries, derived from *Chartreuse*, the mother house of the order. It is synonymous with the German *Karthauser*, Dutch *Kartusier Klooster*, and Italian *Certosa*.
Choir	The part of the church where the monks' stalls were placed, west of the presbytery and east of the pulpitum screen.
Corbel	A decorative stone bracket that projected from a wall-face to support either timber work, a wall-shaft, or the springing of a vault.
Correrie	The house of the lay brethren, originally detached from the main monastery.
Gallery	A timber-framed lean-to structure that connected buildings, a roofed corridor.
Garth	An enclosed space, yard, or paddock, particularly that enclosed by the galleries of a cloister.
Jamb	The side of a door or window frame.
Laver (lavatorium)	The washing-place used by the community before taking meals together in the refectory, supplied with piped water. In Carthusian monasteries, unlike those of other orders, it is small and unadorned.
Lay brother (Frère)	A servant subject to monastic discipline responsible for the day-to-day servicing of the monks or brothers. Used by other orders, the Carthusian lay brother was more closely associated with monastic life than, for instance, Cistercian lay brethren.

Nave	The western part of the monastic church, to the west of the rood screen, used by the lay brethren when they were in the upper house.
Piscina	A stone basin with a drain placed by an altar in which the mass vessels were washed after use.
Presbytery	The eastern part of the monastic church that housed the high altar.
Procurator	The monk or brother who was appointed to be responsible for the lay brethren, guests, and external affairs of the monastery.
Pulpitum	The screen that closed the western end of the monks' choir.
Refectory	The communal dining room, used only on Sundays, major festivals, and on the day of a member of the community's funeral.
Reredos	A panel or screen of wood or stone placed above an altar, often highly decorated and painted. More elaborate instances may have tabernacles filled with figures, simple examples may simply consist of a painting.
Rood Screen	The screen at the east end of the nave, usually with two altars placed either side of a central door.
Sacrist	The monk appointed to be responsible for the upkeep of the chapter house and the liturgical vessels used in the church.
String course	A horizontal moulding used to level up the coursing of rubble walls and to mark the structural divisions of elevations, for instance at the level of window cills or at the base of a parapet.
Suspiral	A valve or tank in a system of water pipes that reduced the pressure in the main to prevent the lead pipes bursting.
Water tower (Age)	A two-storey building, often placed at the centre of the great cloister, which contained a tank that supplied water under pressure to all parts of the monastery.
Vault	The fire-proof stone ceiling of a room or church, supported on corbels or columns, not frequently used by the Carthusians in England after the thirteenth century.

Index

Page numbers in **bold** refer to illustrations